The
Vintage Wood Works
Book Of Ideas
for
PORCH DESIGN

The
Vintage Wood Works
Book Of Ideas
for
PORCH DESIGN

or
How to *Professionally* Design Magnificent Porches,
and Then Order *Exactly* What You'll Need!

J. Gregory Tatsch

A Vintage Wood Works Book

Quinlan, TX 75474
(903) 356-2158   FAX (903) 356-3023

The information in this book is true and complete to the best of our knowledge. All recommendations are made without guarantee on the part of the author or Vintage Wood Works. Information pertaining to structural integrity and design is presented for general reference only. Since specific requirements will vary greatly from one porch to another, we strongly recommend that you consult a knowledgeable architect, building designer, or contractor for assistance in these areas. Also be certain to conform with any local building codes that may be applicable. The author and publisher disclaim all liability incurred with the use of this information.

Printed in the United States of America, Land of the Free!
First Printing, 1994

Dedicated to the memory
of those past Generations,
for whom the Porch
was a focal point of family life ...

...and also to the present
Builders of Porches,
for your efforts
will be enjoyed
by Generations
yet to come.

This is Book One of a two-volume set.
The second book, ***Magnificent Porches Manual***,
tells how to professionally *install* Vintage Wood
Works' porch trim, even if you're *not* a professional.

Take your time.
Enjoy the work as you proceed.

Life is not merely results, however grand,
But mainly the thoughts, the actions, and
The individual moments leading to a goal.

Your added bonus is the joy, the satisfaction,
And the memory of a job well done.
  – Vintage Wood Works' Catalogue #3, 1980

Table of Contents

Preface

Dear Lover of Porches,

We at Vintage Wood Works have always believed that designing and building porches is a most worthwhile endeavor!

Those *"graceful and peaceful surroundings"* to which we com-
mitted ourselves in our very first catalogue are today more
sought after than ever. Indeed, one's happiness, peace of mind,
and even health may be at stake in these hectic times. Anyone
who's ever spent lazy summer evenings on a restful porch un-
derstands this wisdom!

**However, we are also very much aware that the thoughtful
design and skillful construction of even a modest porch is in
danger of becoming a *lost art*.**

Hence this book... our attempt at documenting in a logical, organized (and hopefully enjoyable) manner the knowledge we
have acquired from many years of observation, study, research,
thought, and actual construction of Porches.

We are aware that the success of the finished porch depends
upon much more than proper construction technique, adequate
building materials, or even the "Gingerbread" that we produce
and sell. It is our strong belief that a sensitive understanding
of the various elements of a porch is first necessary. Only then

can one design porches that are at once elegant, balanced, functional, and lasting.

This is *not* to say that we think it takes a professional designer, architect, or contractor to produce professional results. While there are certainly many excellent porches designed and built by these professionals... there is still much that can be learned.

Whether it is your intention to physically build your own porch, only draw the plans, or merely understand the process better, we believe this book can be of help. We are, in fact, writing for both the professional and the homeowner. *Our goal is to share knowledge*! Our hope is that this book will assist you in the study, design, and construction of at least one Magnificent Porch...

Sincerely,

J. Gregory Tatsch
and *The Folks*
at Vintage Wood Works

PS - We would be greatly honored if you would share your thoughts concerning improvements to this book. We will try to incorporate your suggestions into future printings.

Introduction

PORCH... such a simple word, yet so meaningful a place!

For some it conjures up memories of lazy summer afternoon re-
treats. Perhaps your memories are of neighbors... taking their
evening stroll... and stopping by to visit. Maybe you can remember hearing the great political debates waged out on the
front porch by your father and his friends long after you had
been tucked into bed. Could it be that you fell in love while sitting on a porch swing? Or do you remember the magical place
your grandmother's porch was when you played there as a
child? Tall, cool glasses of lemonade... shared secrets... rainy
days... and quiet tree-lined streets... such are the joys of the
American Porch.

Your porch serves as a transitional space, not merely connecting inside to out, but *buffering* the sanctuary, comfort, and order of home from the hustle and bustle of the world beyond. It
offers a place of serenity in those first moments of the day as
you awaken to a cup of coffee or your favorite cereal. Your
porch will also offer a marvelous window on Mother Nature...
shade from the sun... protection from the rain... while you ob-
serve the wonders all around!

As another room to your home, the porch can provide a special place in time for children to be with you... an oasis from the demands inside the home. It's the place that beckons you to sit and put your feet up for a spell as you come in from a long, hectic day.

Without question, a porch sets the stage and feeling of any fine home. First impressions are generally lasting ones. This is true of homes as well as of people. The porch is the means by which your home says *Hello ... and Welcome!*

Reminders

1. We really *are* serious about porches... and we would welcome the opportunity to help you in any way that we can! If questions arise, either during your reading of this book or at a later time, please give us a call at (903) 356-2158.

2. This is Book One of a two-volume set. The second book, *Magnificent Porches Manual,* tells how to professionally **install** Vintage Wood Works' porch trim, even if you're *not* a professional. We will send Book Two *free* upon request when you order any porch trim from us.

3. We'd love to see a picture of *your* Magnificent Porch. Why not keep a photo journal of your progress, and then send us a snapshot of the completed masterpiece?

4. We are always happy to provide a *free* quote on any custom work that you may require. It is quite easy for us to make most requested changes to our standard items, or we can work with you on designs that duplicate existing items you may need to match. We are also often asked to complete special designs for one-of-a-kind projects. Let us know how we can help.

5. But most importantly... have fun!!!

Quick Reference

If you feel you already "know" porches, then you may *not* be planning a cover-to-cover reading of this book...

...but at the very least, please review the *quick reference items* listed below. We feel these are very important points that are often overlooked by even the most experienced builders of porches.

If you *are* planning to read the entire book (and we hope you will!), please refer later to this section as a quick "refresher" on the most important points we will have covered.

This section also provides a good checklist for researching areas that may need attention during any *remodeling* of existing porches.

Quick Reference Items

• The *unturned* portions of Porch Posts must be long enough to accommodate your intended decorative items. Page 36.

• *Half Posts* are available. Page 37.

• *Beams* should be same thickness as Porch Posts. Pages 38-41.

• *Soffit* should be perpendicular to face of Beam. Page 43.

• ALWAYS use *Sloped-top Bottom Rails* outside. Page 49.

• *Subrail* provides several advantages. Page 50.

• *Porch Eave Decorations* provide a dramatic third dimension. Page 52.

• Ways to s t r e t c h your dollars. Page 166.

• Un^{even} Post spacing. Page 169.

• Checklist for review of the front elevation. Page 175.

• Final reminders. Page 190.

Chapter One

An Overview

A Brief History

PORCH n. {L. *porta***, gate} 1.** A covered entrance to a building. **2.** An open or enclosed gallery or room on the outside of a building.

The porch, as most of us think of it, has a long ancestral line. The earliest recognized form is thought to be the *porticos* of ancient Greek architecture. These were towering ornamental roofs supported by massive columns of stone. The evolution of the porch through history has been fueled by the fundamental human need to adapt to, be sheltered from, and yet be a part of our environment. It follows that the various identified architectural types of porches found around the world were developed for their particular localities. Among the more widely recognized forms are the *loggias* of Greece, the *collonades* of Rome, the *verandas* of India, the *stoops* of the Netherlands, the *vestibules* of England, and the *piazzas* of Italy.

Just as America has been a melting pot of human cultures, the same can be said of its porches. Variations of all these porch forms are found repeatedly across America. Few architectural building styles have not benefitted from... and been enriched by... the inclusion of some sort of porch!

With the coming of the Victorian period in architecture, the American porch reached its greatest degree of importance and recognition. Perhaps more than in any other period, the porch was perceived and utilized by the Victorians as an extension of the home's living space. Exuberantly, they embellished their grand creations with intricately detailed woodwork referred to as "gingerbread" or "fretwork". The guidelines established by the Victorians for proportion and propriety in the design of a porch are quite relevant and applicable today. Indeed, our Victorian forefathers had literally decades to perfect their skills and sense of balance in this area of architecture. **We, the present builders of porches, can learn much by careful observation and study of existing examples from this** *Golden Age of Porches!*

On Design

By definition, *design* is the arrangement of parts, details, form, color, etc. so as to produce a complete and artistic whole.

Volumes have been written on the subject of design and its many facets. One can easily and quickly get bogged down with philosophical questions such as *...what is quality? ...what is adequate as opposed to excess? ...or what is proportion?* Rather than contribute to the mass of printed words already accumulated, we will gladly leave these quandaries to our predecessors and take a more practical approach.

Design is at once both an objective *and* subjective process. It is *objective* in that its success is dependant to some extent on the adherence to basic principles, standards, and guidelines. While a castle made of sand may be quite lovely, it will not stand under the next wave.

Design is *subjective* in that it depends on, to a great extent, our own personal aesthetics, tastes, needs... and lest we forget... our own reliable common sense.

Though it may never have occurred to you, design is an exercise you engage in every day. You may not have had an active role in designing the World Trade Center, but you did decide where to hang the pictures on your walls, the color and style of the shoes you choose to wear, or the arrangement of the items on your desk. Both consciously and sub-consciously we make judgement calls concerning virtually everything we encounter. The point is: don't sell yourself short in matters of taste. Perhaps the person most qualified to design *your* porch is the same person who will be living with it... YOU!

Our Parameters

STRUCTURAL INTEGRITY
We will discuss various configurations of the basic porch; however we shall refrain from resolving questions pertaining to structural integrity. Since the specific requirements from one porch to another can vary greatly, we recommend that you consult a knowledgeable architect, building designer, or contractor for assistance in this area. Also be certain to conform with any local building codes that may be applicable.

NEW CONSTRUCTION / PORCH REMODELING
We will focus primarily on *new* porch construction. However, if your porch already exists, a great deal of the information presented throughout this book will still be relevant. Please also see the following section of this Chapter, *Porch Remodeling.*

EXTERIOR PORCHES / INSIDE APPLICATIONS
Further, this book is written from the perspective of the *exterior* porch (including front, back, side, and second story porches). There are, however, a great number of applications for this information *within the home!* For example, it is very dramatic to use porch posts, railings, and Gingerbread to divide a room... to define a sitting area, or to enhance a second floor balcony. Let your imagination be your guide...

Throughout this book we shall be concerned with visual impact, cost effectiveness, ease of installation, permanence, and safety. **Do not hesitate to call us at (903) 356-2158 if you do not understand why we are making a specific suggestion.**

Porch Remodeling

Should you have an **existing** porch that is not exactly the *porch of your dreams*, then a remodeling may be in order...

ASSESSING WHAT IS PRESENT

Often a porch will be of sound construction, but lacking in one or more key components. For example, many more recently constructed porches are missing the *beam* that typically runs directly above the Porch Posts. (Actually, from a structural standpoint, some sort of beam is probably present, but it may be concealed within the space between porch ceiling and roof.) A non-visible beam is a definite handicap if you want to apply decorative components, as we discuss in Chapter II. Or perhaps your porch *does* have a visible beam, but it is *not* of the same width as the porch Posts. Again, this is a hindrance in the proper placement of Gingerbread Decoration.

Your Porch Posts may be to your liking, but positioned such that one or more Posts are directly in front of windows (or even a door). Or you may wish to replace the Posts with a more decorative style. Steps may need re-positioning, or you may choose to add Newel Posts where none previously existed.

On a more major scale, you may want to increase the depth or length of the porch, or add a right-angled section to allow the porch to wrap around a corner of the house. The porch flooring may be in need of repair or replacement, or some of the structural members may need to be replaced or strengthened.

You might choose to add a ceiling, where none previously existed. (Vintage Wood Works has a selection of Beaded Ceiling that is very authentic.) Such an addition facilitates the inclusion of new electrical wiring for lights, ceiling fans, or outlets for Christmas lighting.

In fact, there are many valid reasons to consider remodeling an existing porch rather than starting over from "scratch". Often the job is not nearly as complicated as it would first seem, once the structure is properly analyzed. And, of course, there are often significant savings of time and materials when remodeling rather than starting fresh.

FOR YOUR INITIAL REVIEW
It may be helpful to refer to *Initial Considerations,* **Chapter III,** for a review of points to be considered. Then list all of the existing aspects of your porch that you like and dislike. Be complete. Remember, you are in the "dreaming" stage of planning your remodeling!

Also, please review our **Quick Reference** section for a checklist of areas that may need attention during any *remodeling* of existing porches.

PLAN & ELEVATIONS
Following the instructions of **Chapter III**, draw a floor plan and front and side elevations of the porch *as it presently exists.*

Then, draw a floor plan and front and side elevations of your porch *as you would like for it to be after remodeling.* The sections, **A REVIEW OF THE FRONT ELEVATION** and **THE GINGERBREAD**, both in **Chapter III**, will be helpful. Also, please refer at this time to the sections in **Chapter II** on *Decorative Porch Components* and *Porch Examples* as a refresher on the possibilities available for your porch remodeling.

The Porch and Its Components

Chapter Two

Chapter II is organized into four sections:

Porch Configurations - Drawings, both in "elevation" and in "plan", for a number of general shapes that porches may take.

Structural Porch Components - A "cataloging" of the primary *structural* components that are found on most porches.

Decorative Porch Components - An exploration of the *decorative* items available for your porch. It is, of course, possible for structural members to be decorative, such as with turned Porch Posts.

Porch Examples - A presentation of numerous combinations of components, showing in a comparative way how your porch will appear if these items are used.

Porch Configurations

While there are many possible variations, a porch will tend to follow one of the general shapes illustrated on this and the following eight pages.

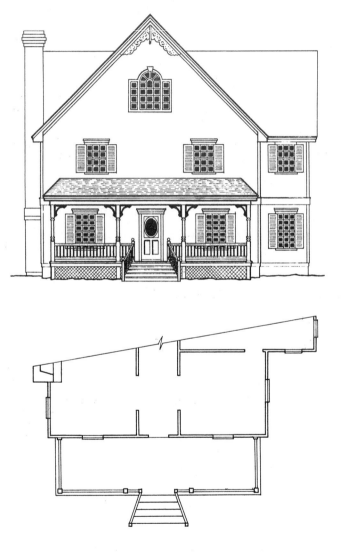

1. The basic rectangular porch.

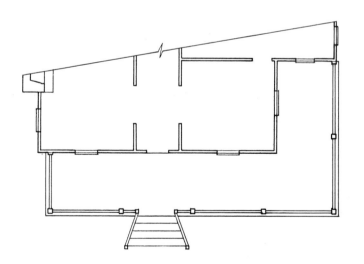

2. The wrap-around porch.

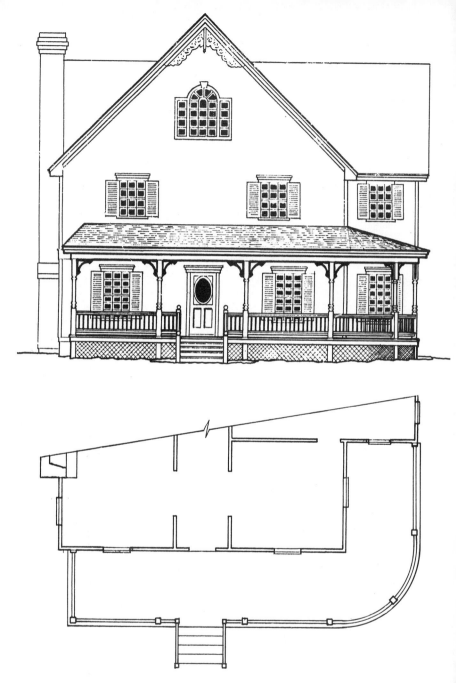

3. Porch with curved section.

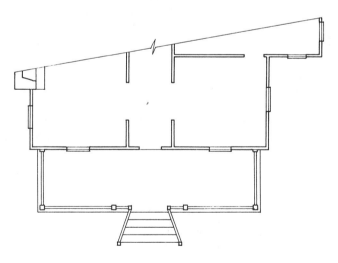

4. Porch with entrance gable.

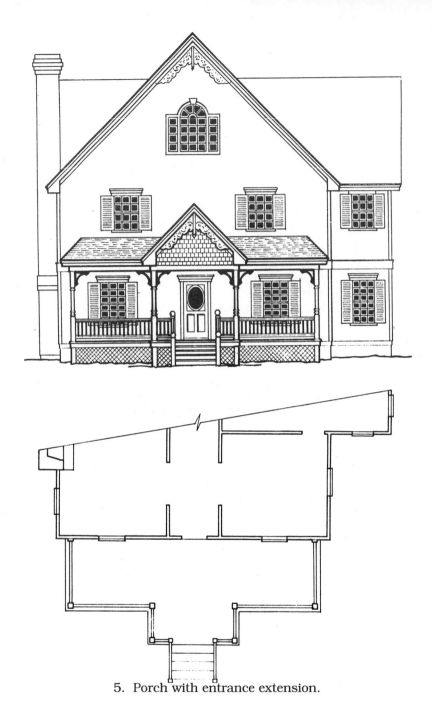

5. Porch with entrance extension.

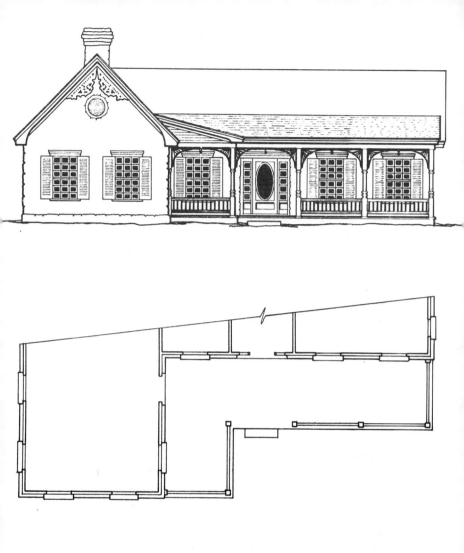

6. An "L" shaped porch.

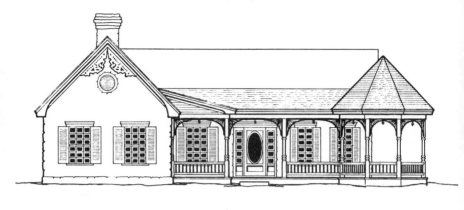

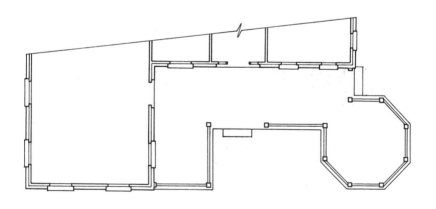

7. Porch with attached gazebo section.

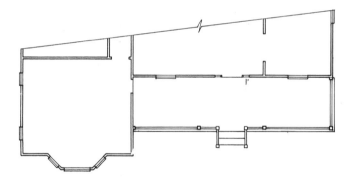

8. The two-story porch.

The second story of a Porch is often shorter. Therefore, it is typical to modify the Decorative Components on the upper level Porch.

Handrail height on the second floor Porch should satisfy local building code, and be at least 36" high.

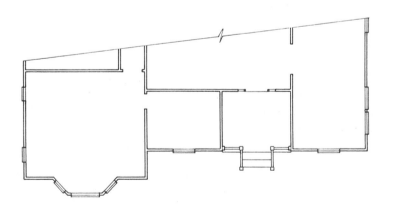

9. The inset porch.

Structural Porch Components

It is *not* within the scope of this book to provide complete instruction in the actual construction of your porch. However, the proper design of porches is not entirely possible without some understanding of the construction process. We feel it is important that you have at least a basic knowledge of the structural aspects, as they greatly effect the overall success of any porch. Further, the misuse of certain structural parts makes it very difficult to apply the decorative components properly. For example, if the front face of the Beam over your Posts is not aligned with the front face of the Posts themselves, it will be more difficult to properly use Post Face Brackets, should you so desire.

Following is a "cataloging" of the primary *structural* components that are found on most porches. (Obviously, it is also possible for structural members to be decorative, such as with turned Porch Posts.)

THE PORCH PLATFORM

Obviously, the porch must have a floor of some sort, but also you need a foundation and, depending upon the type of foundation, there may be floor framing. We will discuss the following components of what we call the porch *platform:*

1. Foundation
   To support the structure above.

2. Floor framing (if applicable)
   Wooden floor joists to support the floor.

3. Floor
   May be wood, tile, concrete, stone, or other materials.

Please seek professional assistance in determining the proper foundation. The most important consideration with any foundation is that it be stable; able to withstand any movement the underlying ground may experience for many years to come. Frost heave (the tendency of frozen ground to push upward) must always be addressed where the ground freezes in winter. Most porch foundations will be of either *Pier & Beam* or *Concrete Slab* construction.

Pier and Beam foundations are typically used where a wood floor is desired. These foundations support 3/4" or thicker flooring (decking) above a structural wooden framework (floor joists). The joists are supported by beams (girders) that lay across the tops of short posts or columns (piers). See illustration #10. Each pier typically sits atop a concrete pad (footing) in the ground. The joist framework is often supported directly by the piers, as shown in illustration #11. Joists and Beams should be of pressure treated lumber to withstand the moist conditions they are subjected to.

To allow proper water drainage, the foundation and joists should be built with a slight slope towards the front of the porch. Also, the floor boards must run from the front to the back of the porch. This will allow water to run down the boards and off the front of the porch. Therefore, it will be necessary to install blocking between the joists, as shown below.

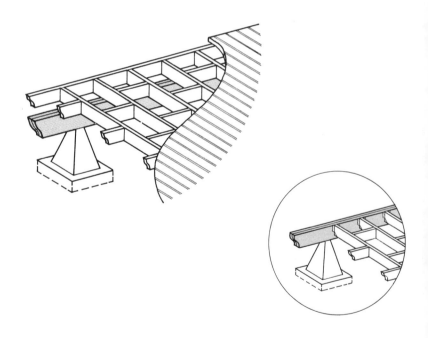

10 & 11.   Pier and Beam foundations.

The Concrete Slab foundation (illustration #12) is typically a solid poured-in-place concrete structure. The resulting concrete floor may be used directly, or tile, stone, brick, or other masonry type finished floor may be applied over the concrete (in which case, it is very important to lower the finished height of the concrete to allow for the *installed* thickness of this floor). The concrete slab, as it is commonly called, is strengthened with steel bars or wire running through its core. The slab is generally 3" to 6" thick. Concrete beams (footings) 10" to 16" wide and 12" to 36"deep typically are placed under its perimeter and occasionally through its length or width depending upon the size of the slab. Most people, unless they have experience in this area, will contract to have a professional "pour the slab".

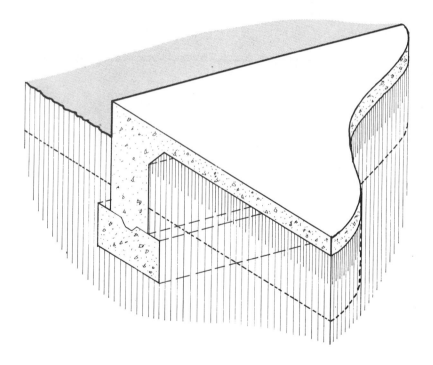

12. Concrete Slab foundation.
(Dotted line represents "frost line".)

Floor framing

If you are planning a Pier and Beam Foundation, then you will need to decide upon the size and spacing of your beams and joists. It is always preferable to err on the side of larger and closer, for you will want your porch floor to feel (and to be) very sturdy! Please seek professional advice in determining these important factors.

Where the floor joists meet the wall of the building to which the porch is to be attached, it is typical to have a ledger board, as shown in illustration #13. This ledger board is fastened horizontally to the building, so as to receive the ends of the floor joists. It, as well as the rest of the floor framing, should be of pressure treated lumber, as mentioned earlier. *This ledger must, of course, be fastened securely into the structure of the building, as it will support considerable weight.* We recommend the use of steel Joist Hangers as the method of attaching joists to the ledgers, both for their ease of installation, and for their strength.

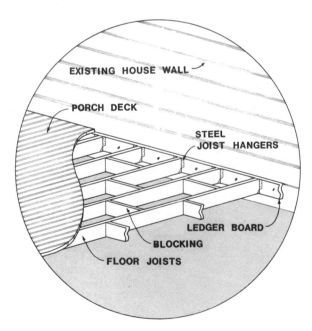

13. Ledger board fastened directly to the building.

The floor

Your choice of floor type will depend upon the type of foundation you choose (or vice versa). Pier and Beam foundations are typically used for wood floors, while masonry floors are normally laid over concrete slab foundations.

Regardless of the material chosen for your floor, you should design your porch so that the front and side edges of the floor will be inside the line of the roof overhang. This will, obviously, keep your porch floor drier.

Wood floors

Providing your joist blocking is spaced closely enough for adequate support, a very traditional wood floor can be made of 1 by 4 lumber. Many "old-timers" feel this lumber should *not* be "flooring" (with tongue & groove or shiplapped edges), as this will tend to trap moisture. Rather, they favor a premium grade of square-edged lumber, nailed down edge to edge. The resulting cracks between boards allow moisture to fall through to the ground below. These same old-timers avoid the use of pressure treated lumber for flooring, as it often warps badly. It would seem prudent, however, to use some sort of water repellant treatment, and for best results this should be applied to all four sides of each floor board prior to installation. If such treatment is used, be sure to allow boards to dry for several days before installation.

For any wood floor, the individual boards should run from the front to the back of the porch, as mentioned above. This will allow water to run down the boards and off the front of the porch. If the boards were to run the length of the porch, the cracks between boards would impede the flow of water! And as also mentioned above, be sure that there is a *slope* from the front of the porch to the back.

Obviously, a premium grade of porch decking paint is required for any wood floor! Also, it is always a good idea to keep shrubbery trimmed well back from wooden porches, as this will keep the porch drier.

Masonry floors

As mentioned above, be sure to allow for the installed thickness of the tile, brick, stone, etc. that you may wish to apply over your concrete slab.

THE POSTS

Full Posts

Porch Posts extend from the top of the porch floor to the bottom of the Beam. Ideally they are spaced uniformly at the exposed edge or edges of the porch. Vintage Wood Works' Posts are available in several styles, diameters, and lengths.

A turned porch Post includes three areas: the *top square*, the *turning*, and the *base square*, as shown in illustration #14. The top square is the unturned portion at the top of the Post. Its finished length after installation must be sufficient to allow the decorative components (Spandrel, Brackets, etc.) to fit entirely on this flat area. The turning is, of course, the decorative mid-section of the Post. And the base square is the unturned bottom portion of the Post. Its length after installation must, of course, allow the Handrail to fit entirely on its flat surface.

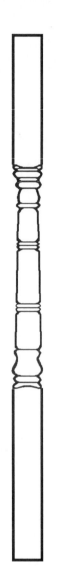

14. Turned Porch Post

15. Half Post used at a wall.

Half Posts

Half Porch Posts are merely full Posts that have been split lengthwise. They have flat backsides, for use against walls. (Illustration #15.) Vintage Wood Works provides Half Posts already split and ready to install.

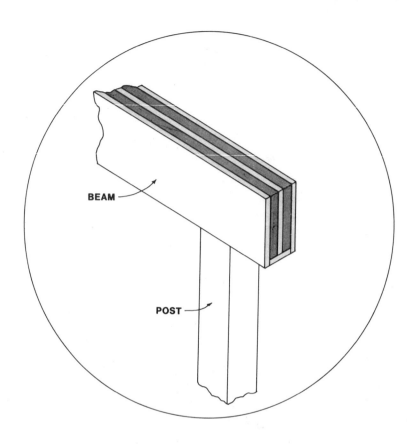

16. Beam should be the same thickness as your Porch Posts.

THE BEAM

The Beam is the structural framing member that spans across the tops of the Posts. (Illustration #16.) It must be sized to transfer and support the weight of the roof structure.

While it is common practice *not* to do so, we highly recommend that the Beam be laminated in such a manner that its finished *thickness* is identical to that of the Posts supporting it. (Please study illustrations #17-21.) This will eliminate an awkward and unsightly offset between the faces of the Posts and of the Beam. Equally important, it allows easier and more graceful application of your Gingerbread components.

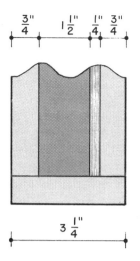

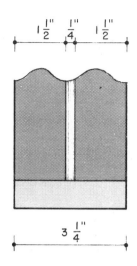

17. (left) Using two 3/4" thick *face* pieces, with a solid *core* consisting of one 1-1/2" thick piece of lumber and one 1/4" layer of plywood to match a 3-1/4" thick Porch Post. This is the recommended configuration (due to the availability of presentable 3/4" lumber), *if* strength is adequate for the spans (between Posts) involved.

18. (right) Using two 1-1/2" thick *face* pieces, and one 1/4" layer of plywood is an alternative way to build a laminated Beam that matches a 3-1/4" thick Porch Post. This is the recommended configuration *only if* extra strength is required, due to the spans between Posts.

Illustrations #17-21 show several ways that standard lumber and plywood can be used to achieve Beam thicknesses equal to standard modern Porch Post thicknesses.

Obviously, it is desirable to use a very good grade of lumber for any *exposed face* of your Beam. *Generally, it is easier (and less expensive) to find presentable facing lumber in 3/4" thickness, rather than in 1-1/2" thickness.*

Also, while not often seen because of the extra time involved, it is possible to *miter* (45° cut) the edges of your lumber, so that the seam between individual pieces is almost invisible.

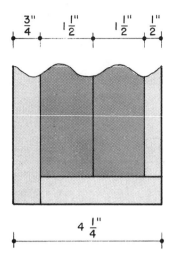

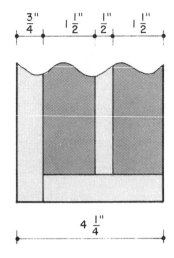

19. (left) Using one 3/4" thick *face* piece, and one 1/2" thick *face* piece, with a solid core of two 1-1/2" thick piece of lumber. This will match a 4-1/4" thick Porch Post. This is the recommended configuration (due to the availability of presentable 3/4" lumber), but will require also locating presentable 1/2" thick lumber. (Any cabinet shop should be able to plane down 3/4" thick boards to your required 1/2".) Of course, 1/2" plywood could be used, but care must be taken to choose a grade of plywood that will match your other lumber after painting.

20. (right) Using one 3/4" thick *face* piece, and one 1-1/2" thick *face* piece, together with a core of one 1-1/2" thick piece of lumber, and one 1/2" layer of plywood is an alternative way to build a laminated Beam that matches a 4-1/4" thick Porch Post. This is the recommended configuration ***only if*** a suitable 1/2" face material *cannot* be located for the configuration shown in illustration #19, as it is difficult to procure 1-1/2" lumber that has a presentable face.

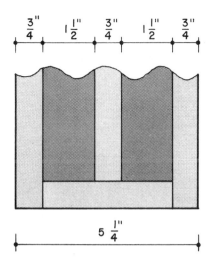

21. Using two 3/4" thick *face* pieces, with a solid *core* of two 1-1/2" thick pieces of lumber and one 3/4" piece of lumber. This will match a 5-1/4" thick Porch Post.

THE ROOF STRUCTURE

We recommend that you seek professional assistance in determining a proper roof structure for your porch. Type of roofing material, snow load, rafter and ceiling joists sizes, etc. are best determined by an experienced person.

1. Rafters

Rafters are structural members that are set perpendicular to and on top of the Beam. They extend at a slope up to the face of the building. Rafters are typically spaced 16" or 24" apart along the length of the porch. The *Pitch* (slope) of a roof is defined as "the number of feet the roof rises *vertically* for each 12 feet of *horizontal* measure". Hence, a 4/12 Pitch roof will rise 4" for every 12" it travels. If a porch is 8' deep from the face of the building to the Beam, and the Rafters are installed with a 4/12 Pitch, then the Rafters will intersect the *face* of the building 32" above the porch Beam.

2. Ceiling Joists

Ceiling Joists are structural members placed on top of the Beam next to each Rafter. They extend perpendicular to the Beam to the face of the building, horizontal and level.

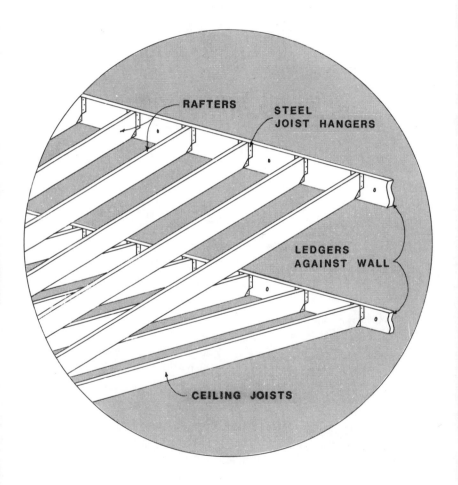

22. Connecting the porch to an existing wall.

3. Ledgers (Ribbon Boards)
Ledgers are boards fastened horizontally to the building so as to receive the ends of either the rafters or ceiling joists. We recommend the use of steel Joist Hangers as the method of fastening Joists and Rafters to the Ledgers, both for their ease of installation, and for their strength. See illustration #22.

4. Fascia Boards
Fascia Boards (illustration #23) are applied across the ends of the Rafter Tails (the section of the Rafter that extends beyond the Beam creating the roof overhang).

5. Soffit
The Soffit (illustration #23) is the material applied to the bottom of the Rafter ends serving to "box in" the overhang. If the Soffit is installed perpendicular to the face to the Beam, it will be much easier to add Gingerbread Trim in this area. See PORCH EAVE DECORATION later in this Chapter.

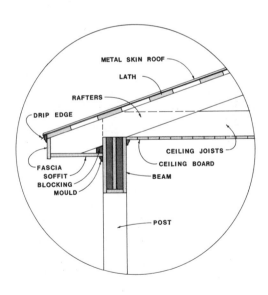

23. Cross section of lower eave of a typical porch.

6. Ceiling

Ceiling material is applied to the bottom edges of the ceiling joists. There are many different materials available for ceilings; from plain plywood to the highly authentic and decorative Beaded Ceiling Boards supplied by Vintage Wood Works, as shown below.

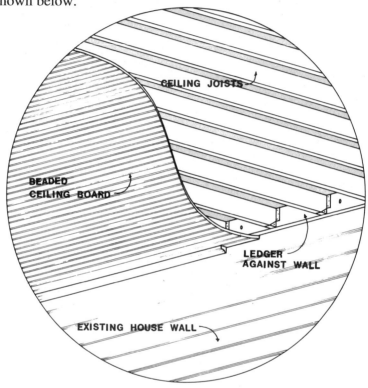

24. Beaded Ceiling Board - both authentic & very decorative.

7. Roof Decking

Roof Decking (illustration #25) is applied to the top edges of the Rafters to provide rigidity to the roof structure and a nailing base for the roofing material. The two common types of decking are sheets of plywood or lath (1x4's or 1x6's applied perpendicular to the Rafters, spaced 12" - 20" apart). Lath is most often used under metal roofing, to allow space to dissipate any condensate that may form on the underside of the metal. Otherwise, the metal roofing may in time rust through from below.

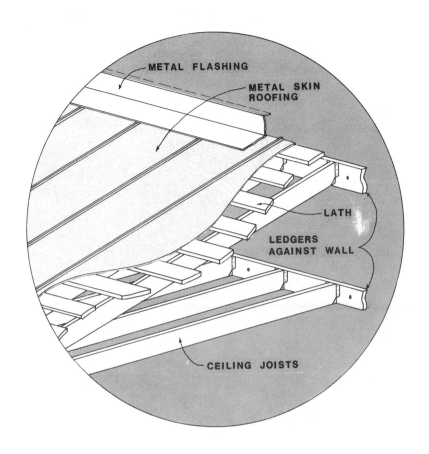

25. Cut-away view of the porch roof
(with lath boards and metal roofing material).

8. Roofing

There are numerous roofing systems available. Among them are metal skin, composition shingle, wood shakes or shingles, tile, and slate. Typically, the porch roof will match the roofing material of the building to which it is attached.

Decorative Porch Components

We will briefly define each type of decorative component, and will explore how each of these items relate to one another, and to the overall design of your porch.

Please also see Chapter IV, **Ordering Materials**, for additional information on each type of decorative component. (That Chapter's organization follows the outline set forth for this section.)

Also, please be aware that Vintage Wood Works welcomes the opportunity to provide *variations* on any of our decorative porch components. We will also be happy to quote purely custom work. This service is particularly valuable if you're planning to match existing trim.

We can categorize the Gingerbread (decorative) components of the porch into four broad groups:

1. The Newel Posts

2. The Balustrade
   Hand and bottom Rails, together with
   turned or sawn Balusters

3. Post Top Items
   Spandrels, Running Trims, Brackets, Etc.

4. Porch Eave Decoration
   Belt Course Brackets, Post Face Brackets, Etc.

THE NEWEL POSTS

Newel Posts extend from the top of the porch floor (or step) to a height sufficient to allow adequate space in which to attach the end of a balustrade. Newels are most commonly used where the balustrades will change direction or will end, such as at the steps (illustration #26, below).

26. Newel Posts terminating Balustrade at either side of steps.

In the event that the space between Porch Posts is fairly long, Newel Posts can be placed between each pair of Porch Posts to add visual interest, as shown here.

27. Newel Post between pair of Porch Posts.

THE BALUSTRADE

A *Balustrade* is a handrail assembly that extends from one post to another. The various components that make up a Balustrade are:

1. Bottom Rail

Because of high exposure and vulnerability to rain, an improperly designed Bottom Rail will have a much shorter life than the rest of your porch. If it does not shed water properly, it will even jeopardize the Balusters attached to it. Vintage Wood Works' Sloped-Top Bottom Rail provides proper water drainage, simple installation, low cost and authentic traditional styling. It will accommodate both Turned and Sawn Balusters from 3/4" to 2 1/2" wide. Please see illustration #28.

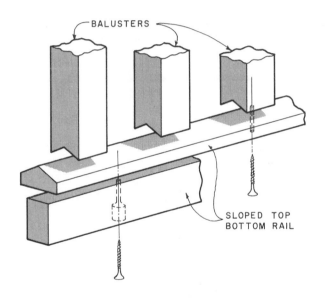

28. Sloped-Top Bottom Rail provides proper water drainage.

2. Balusters

Balusters are the vertical, spaced members between the Bottom Rail and Handrail (or Subrail, if this is used). Sawn Balusters are available in different styles and thicknesses, and in various lengths. Turned Balusters are also available in a variety of styles, with a selection of widths and lengths.

3. Subrail

The Subrail (illustration #29) is the member that runs across the tops of, and is fastened to, the Balusters. Its use simplifies installation, while allowing the Handrail a more substantial look at nominal additional cost.

An added bonus is the ease with which you can *pre-paint* Subrails in an *accent color*, providing a pin-striping effect upon installation! This is, of course, much easier to accomplish with a separate Subrail, as opposed to painting such a pin-stripe directly on a portion of the Handrail. (Multiple color schemes are always easier with pre-painting of separate components.)

We strongly recommend the use of Subrail for all porches...

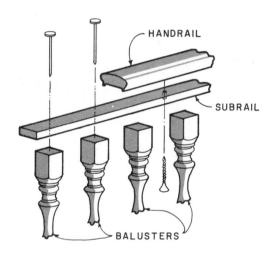

29. Subrail simplifies installation of Balusters.

4. Handrail (Cap Rail)

The Handrail is applied on top of the Subrail, thereby concealing the nails or screws used to hold the Baluster tops. By screwing *up* through the *bottom* of the Subrail into the *bottom* of the Handrail, all exposed hardware is eliminated! *The width of the channel in the bottom of your Handrail must, of course, match the width of the Subrail used.*

5. Integral Spandrel

An integral Spandrel is occasionally used between the Handrail and the Balusters. It is most applicable when a fancier Balustrade is desired. It is also a most effective way to increase the overall height of a balustrade. Typically the height of these integral Spandrels would not exceed eight inches. Please see illustrations below.

30.

31.

POST TOP and PORCH EAVE DECORATION

Next we'll be discussing the various types of components found at the top of a porch. As we discuss these areas, please refer back to this drawing if it helps you understand this portion of a typical porch.

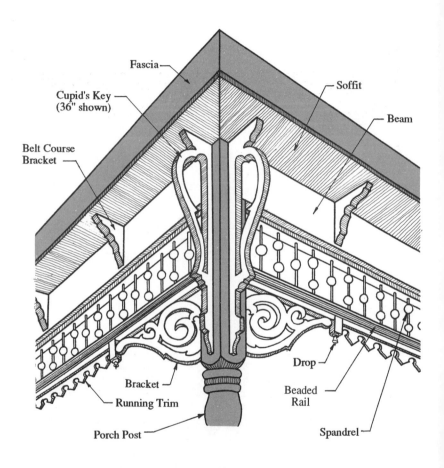

32.

Overhanging eave... with substantial Beam below... Post Face and Belt Course Brackets in at least 1-1/2" thickness... these are classical elements of the traditional porch.

POST TOP ITEMS
We define *Post top items* as all of the decorative components that are used around and between the tops of the Porch Posts.

1. Spandrels
Spandrels are the row of Balls & Dowels, Spindles, or Cutwork. They are installed directly below the Beam, extending from one Post Top to another (illustration #33). If the distance between posts is too long for one Spandrel panel, a Drop (2" square piece with a turned end) can be used between multiple Spandrels. Drops are available in custom lengths to accommodate the Spandrel's height. *All Vintage Wood Works' Spandrels are available in custom lengths.*

Types of Spandrels include:

• *Fretwork Spandrels* - with scrollwork integrated into the design.

• *Ball & Dowel Spandrels* - with or without scrollwork centers.

• *Spindle Spandrels* - again with or without scrollwork centers.

• *Ball & Spindle Spandrels* - combination of both Ball & Dowel and Spindles, used alternately.

• *Spool Spandrels* - with heavier "spool" Spindles.

• *Cut Out Spandrels* - with only scrollwork, and no Balls & Dowels or Spindles.

• *Traditional Spandrels* - with heavier turned Spindles.

• *Fan Spandrels* - with Fan Brackets integrated into the design.

• *Cookie Cutter Spandrels* - solid boards with holes and/or cutouts to form a repeating design.

Additionally, any of these types of Spandrels can have several options:

- *Heavier* top and/or bottom rails.

- *Gallery Rails* (small Ball & Dowel or Spindle Spandrels) - built into the Spandrel.

- *Small Scrollwork Spandrels* - built into the Spandrel.

The type of Spandrel chosen is a matter of personal taste. It is very appropriate to mix types between Spandrels and Brackets. For example, a Ball & Dowel Spandrel is fine with a cutwork Bracket.

33. You can use *Two* Spandrels at the Post tops, shown here separated by our Beaded Rail.

2. Brackets

Brackets are applied beneath the Spandrel (illustration #34) or directly beneath the Beam, if a Spandrel is *not* used. They are centered against the side of the Posts. Brackets can, of course, be mounted either vertically or horizontally.

Types of Brackets include:

- *Fan Brackets*

- *Regular Brackets*

- *Fret Brackets*

- *Corbels* - Because they are dimensionally larger than Brackets, Corbels are normally used on larger scale porches.

The type of Bracket chosen is also a matter of personal taste.

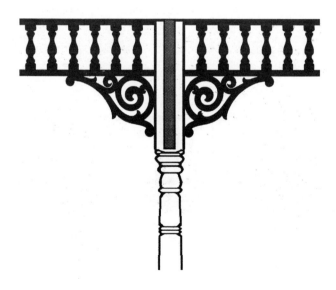

34. Brackets below Spandrels enhance your porch!

3. Running Trims

Running Trims are characterized by their repeating pattern. They can be used *below* Spandrels, running from Bracket to Bracket (illustration #35), or they can be used *without* Brackets (illustration #36). Often a Drop (2" square piece with a turned end) is positioned at the end of the Bracket, with the Running Trim then butting into the other side of the Drop. A very nice extra touch is to order your Running Trim with a moulded Top Rail attached. This will give additional detailing to the finished porch at very little extra expense, and will simplify installation.

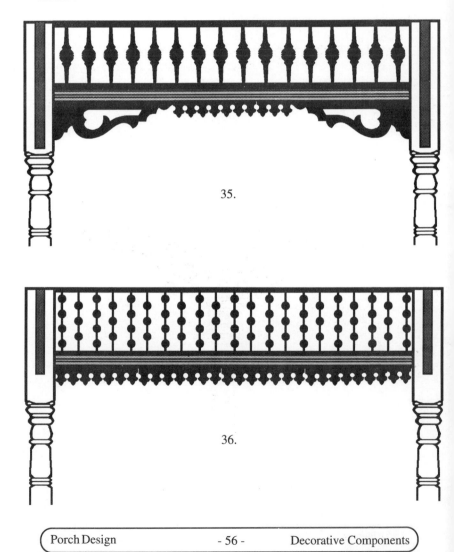

35.

36.

4. Beaded Rails

The use of Beaded Rail is often called for when a more substantial effect is desired. Normally this piece will run from post to post, below the Spandrels. Please see illustrations below.

A Beaded Rail will add to the visual mass of the bottom rail of the Spandrel. It will also set off your Brackets, providing additional definition, texture, and interest. The Beaded Rail's width should *exceed* the width of the bottom rail of the Spandrel.

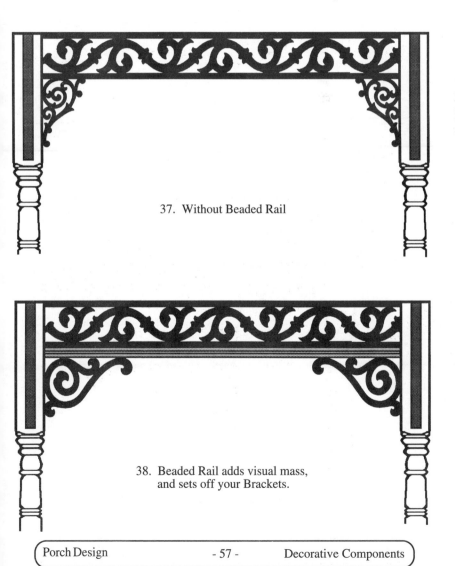

37. Without Beaded Rail

38. Beaded Rail adds visual mass,
    and sets off your Brackets.

5. Medallions

Medallions provide additional decoration in the Post Top area of your porch. They are positioned against the side of each Post, directly below the Beam (illustration #39). Traditionally, they are only used in conjunction with Spandrels, or between two closely spaced Posts. When used with Spandrels, the Medallion must be of the same depth as the Spandrel, as the Spandrel will butt against the Medallion. Often a Drop is used as a transitional element between Medallion and Spandrel. When Medallions are used between pairs of closely spaced Posts, they take the place of Spandrels, and will often also replace the Brackets.

39. Medallion used between pairs of Porch Posts.

PORCH EAVE DECORATION
*Of all the decorations used on your porch, Eave Decorations will probably create the most dramatic effect because they introduce a **third dimension** of depth to the design.*

Unfortunately, they are also the most often overlooked decorative components. However, without Eave Decoration, an otherwise elegant porch can appear "flat" and without character. We are sometimes asked, after a porch is completed, why it does not seem "authentic"? More often than not, our finding is that the Eave Decoration is missing!

1. Post Face Brackets
Post Face Brackets are installed in the corner of the intersection of the Soffit (horizontal board in front of the Beam) and the Beam. Please see illustrations below. They are centered on, and extend down the front face of the Post Tops. Typically, these special Brackets are 1-1/4" or more in thickness, and are fairly long relative to their width.

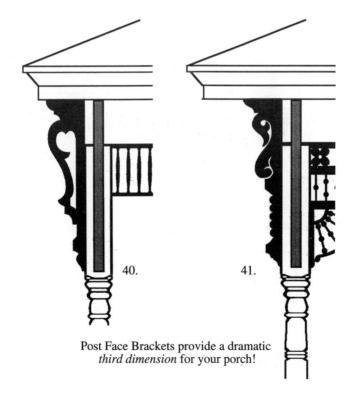

40.   41.

Post Face Brackets provide a dramatic
third dimension for your porch!

2. Belt Course Brackets (Eave Brackets)

Belt Course Brackets are uniformly spaced along the eave of the porch, between Post Face Brackets, if these are present. Like Post Face Brackets, they are installed in the corner of the intersection of the Soffit and Beam.

42. Belt Course Brackets also add this third dimension.

It is also very effective to use Belt Course Brackets in pairs, as shown below. This is particularly appropriate when the Posts are spaced farther apart, or when a slightly more formal arrangement is desired.

43. Belt Course Brackets are often used in pairs.

For a more *substantial* eave decoration, you can use Corbels (thicker Brackets) in place of standard Belt Course Brackets. The drawing below shows this approach.

44. Small Corbels work well as Eave Brackets.

3. Running Trims as Appliques
These can be applied directly to the exposed, outside face of the Beam. They can be used *in conjunction with* the Belt Course Brackets (placed between the Belt Course Brackets) as shown here.

45.   For extra effect, add Running Trim as an applique to the Beam.

Or applied Running Trims can be used *in lieu of* Belt Course Brackets, as shown below. While this treatment is very decorative, the absence of Belt Course Brackets diminishes the third dimensional effect we feel is so important!

46. Running Trim used in lieu of Belt Course Brackets.

4. Appliques used on the face of the Beam

As with Running Trims, these can be applied directly to the exposed, outside face of the Beam. Again, they can be used *in conjunction with* the Belt Course Brackets (placed between the Belt Course Brackets), or they can be used *in lieu of* Belt Course Brackets, but then at the risk of diminishing the "third dimension" effect.

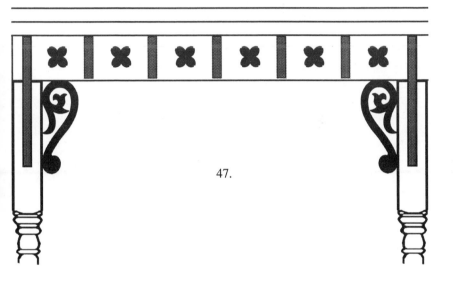

47.

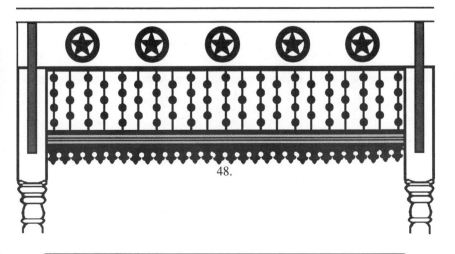

48.

Porch Examples

Since "a picture *is* worth a thousand words", we're including here numerous examples of porches. View each example as a *complete* porch, but also use these illustrations for *comparison*. By showing many variations on the same theme, we've tried to provide the answers to such questions as:

"What is the best Baluster spacing for my porch?"
"How tall should my Handrail be?"
"Do I prefer Sawn or Turned Balusters?"

COOKBOOK APPROACH
This chapter can easily serve as "cookbook" for "whipping up" your own special porch. We've purposely duplicated the same few basic porches, changing only the decorative items. Thus, the Balustrade sections, Spandrels, etc. from one example will likely interchange with another porch. We encourage you to make photocopies of porch examples with features you like. Cut these *features* out, and hold over other porches, thereby creating your own unique porch.

For example, assume you like everything *except* the Balustrade of one of these examples. Locate your favorite Balustrade sections from among our examples. Copy, cut them out, and hold each over your favorite porch's Balustrade. With this "cut and paste" approach you can "see" your porch before you build!

PRODUCT LISTING
You can easily recreate any porch (or portion thereof) shown here, since all decorative items are readily available from Vintage Wood Works. We've listed, with each porch example, the Vintage Wood Works' items used to create that porch. (Many Brackets are shown *without* frames, but we *do* feel frames are cost effective options for your Brackets!)

If you'd like to duplicate a porch (or portion thereof), please discuss your order with Vintage Wood Works (903-356-2158). We'll determine if we need to make slight modifications to any items to assure a perfect fit on *your* porch.

Also, please don't hesitate to discuss ideas *you* may have for modifications or custom work. **Our goal is to provide cost effective items that create *exactly* the porch of your dreams!**

TO SCALE (Well, Almost!)
We've tried diligently to maintain a consistent scale for the illustrations in this chapter. If you buy the listed products from Vintage, and use them as shown in the illustration, you'll be able to stand back and admire a porch that looks very, very close to what you see in the illustration!

In an effort to include many illustrations, and still publish this book during our lifetimes, we have taken small liberties with the sizing of a few items. A Bracket listed as 24" long may actually scale out to only 23". In our opinion, these slight variations will not change the overall look of a given porch.

INTERPRETING TWO-DIMENSIONAL ILLUSTRATIONS
These porch illustrations are presented in "two dimensions"; that is, as viewed directly from the front (straight on). Thus, for *Post Face Brackets* (which are mounted to the *faces* of the Posts), you'll see the *full outline* of *only* the Bracket that shows to the *side* of the porch. For all other Post Face Brackets, you're seeing only the front *edge*, not the flat side of the Bracket. We represent this edge as a long, gray rectangle. That's what you'd see looking straight at the front of a porch.

Likewise, Belt Course Brackets, installed perpendicular to the face of the Beams, are shown as a gray *edge*. Please remember, as you study these illustrations, that the most successful porches *do* present themselves *in real life* in three dimensions!

To help you understand our *two*-dimensional examples, we are first providing, immediately following, a porch drawn in *three*-dimensions; that is, as viewed from an angle, rather than "straight on". It's not as easy to see exactly what a *specific* item will look like from this perspective drawing (as it's sometimes called) but it will help you understand the overall relationship that various components have to one another.

And, as always, if there is anything that you do not understand, please remember that the folks at Vintage Wood Works are ready and eager to help. We'll be glad to discuss any illustrations, and to answer your questions.

Just give us a call at **(903) 356-2158**.

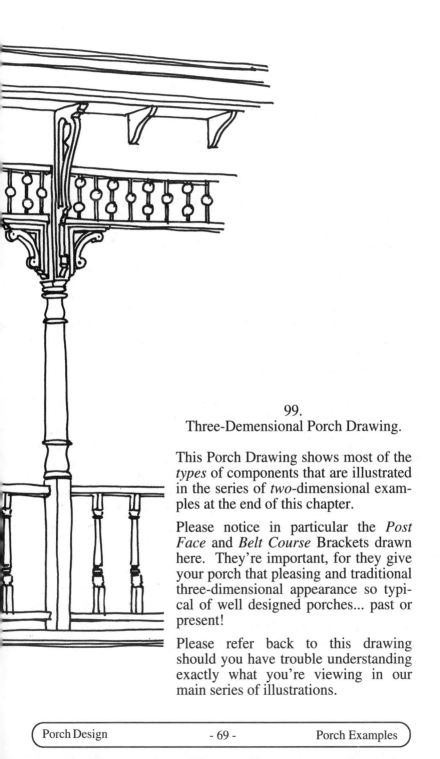

99.
Three-Demensional Porch Drawing.

This Porch Drawing shows most of the *types* of components that are illustrated in the series of *two*-dimensional examples at the end of this chapter.

Please notice in particular the *Post Face* and *Belt Course* Brackets drawn here. They're important, for they give your porch that pleasing and traditional three-dimensional appearance so typical of well designed porches... past or present!

Please refer back to this drawing should you have trouble understanding exactly what you're viewing in our main series of illustrations.

Cross References
(by page number)

first by specific usage, *then* by Product Number

for the Porch Examples in this Chapter

We offer here *two* complete Cross References to the porch examples in the last section of this chapter. First, each porch component is indexed, *by specific usage*, to the page that illustrates that usage. A *second* cross reference, *by Vintage Wood Works Product Number,* immediately follows.

For example, let's say you've decided on Traditional style turned Balusters, but are unsure which "on center" spacing you prefer. In the *Specific Usage Cross Reference*, first look under *Balusters*, and then under *Traditional*. There you will find a listing of examples in this chapter that illustrate various spacing options using the Traditional style of Baluster.

By extension, you can also use the *Specific Usage Cross Reference* to find illustrations that serve your purpose, even though they may actually use slightly different items. In the example above, if the Baluster style you're interested is *not* shown at the spacing you want, use this cross reference to locate other Baluster styles that may be presented in that particular spacing.

Or, if you want to see porch examples using a *particular item* from the Vintage Wood Works Catalogue, refer to the *Product Number Cross Reference.*

And please remember... it's easy to copy pages from this book, then mix and match *portions* of those pages to create additional Porch examples of your own.

Specific Usage Cross Reference
(by page number)
for the Porch Examples in this Chapter

Balustrade
BEADED RAIL
1-1/2"x2-1/2" size, pp.105, 117, 118, 120, 143

BOTTOM RAILS
Sloped Top Bottom Rail, pp.83, and many others

HANDRAILS / SUBRAILS
P2 Handrail
    with Subrail, pp.83, and many others
    without Subrail, p.161
P3 Handrail, pp.89, and many others
S Handrail, p.99
SR2 Subrail, pp.83, and many others
SR3 Subrail, pp.89, and many others

SAWN BALUSTERS
Classical Urn Style
    12" o.c., p.128
    14" o.c., p.124
Heart & Fleur Style
    spaced together, pp.86, 116, 117
Spear Style
    alternating with 1x3, p.88
    spaced together, pp.83, 84, 119, 125
    spaced with 3" between, p.85
    two, used in center of 1 x 3 flat balusters, p.122
    11" o.c., p.109
    14" o.c., p.108
SB# 5 Style
    shortened, p.143
    spaced together, pp.140, 142
    8" o.c., p.135
    with plain 1x3, p.123

Beams

Porch Eave Decorations

APPLIQUES

Arrow Head Running Trim
    3-3/8" size, pp.92, 115, 123
Circle Star Applique, p.131
Dogwood Applique
    used with Belt Course, p.122
    used without Belt Course, p.129
Fleur Running Trim,
    3-3/8" size, p.88
    5" size, with Belt Course, p.93
    7" size, without Belt Course, p.89
Star Applique, 7" size, p.130
Wistaria Spandrel, 5" size, pp.90, 91

BELT COURSE BRACKETS

7-1/2" size
    4" o.c., p.95
    6" o.c., p.94
    12" o.c., pp.83, and many others
    12" o.c., used in pairs, p.96
    18" o.c., p.97
    24" o.c., pp.93, 98
301   Classic Corbel, horizontal, 12" o.c., p.105
301S Small Classic Corbel, horizontal, 10" o.c., pp.100, 101-104
Little Belt Course, 12" o.c., p.99
Little Swan, 12" o.c., p.87
No Belt Course Bracket, p.108

POST FACE BRACKETS

23" Cupid's Key, pp.83, and many others
31" Cupid's Key, pp.90, and many others
36" Cupid's Key, pp.89, 116, 117
Bird of Paradise, pp.86, 87
Citrus Top Corbel, p.157
Ruffled Swan, p.154
Swan's Neck, p.94
No Post Face Bracket, pp.93, 108

Porch Posts

Post Top Items

EXTENDER
1-1/2" x 1-1/2" size, p.121
1-1/2" x 2" size, pp.102, 143

MEDALLIONS
Shell, 18" size, p.114
Tulip, p.113
Victorian Circle, p.115

RUNNING TRIMS
Fleur Running Trim
    3-3/8" size
        between Brackets, pp.103, 120
        under Spandrels, p.131
    7" size, with SR#4 Bracket, p.119
Picket
    3-3/8" size, under Spandrel, pp.140, 142
Vine, p.135
Wistaria, see Appliques

SPANDRELS
Anna Marie, pp.137, 139
Dogwood Spandrel, p.154
Eloise, pp.115, 138
Lily Langtry, p.123
Mary Elizabeth, p.159
SB#5, shortened, pp.140-142
Willow Spandrel, p.113
Wistaria Spandrel
    6-1/2" size, pp.87, 105, 118
    8-1/2" size, pp.124-125, 128
3-1/2" Ball & Dowel, p.160
4-1/2" Ball & Dowel, p.88
5" Ball & Dowel, p.133
6" Ball & Dowel, pp.109, 134, 154
7" Ball & Dowel, pp.107, 151
7" Spool Spandrel, pp.104, 144
8" Ball & Dowel, pp.129, 143
8-3/4" Ball & Dowel, pp.86, 95, 155
9" Ball & Dowel, pp.126, 136, 158
9-1/2" Spindle, pp.132, 137

Product Number Cross Reference
(by page number)
for the Porch Examples in this Chapter

121-075 Classic Porch Post 5"x96", 32" base, pp.106-107,
            136-137
121-084 Classic Porch Post 6"x96", 32" base, pp.108-109
121-100 New Orleans Porch Post 5"x96", 36" base, p.93

1231 FB#1 Bracket, p.88
1232n11 FB#2 Bracket, pp.108-109
1233 FB#3 Bracket, pp.114, 124
1234 Arch Bracket, p.133
1235n12 FB#4 Bracket, p.107
1238 Stockbridge Bracket, p.146
1239 Archredeux Bracket, p.147
1241 FB#7 Bracket, p.134
1242 FB#6 Bracket, p.89
1243n10 FB#8 Bracket, p.144
1243n12 FB#8 Bracket, p.145
1247 Arch Bracket, pp.106, 136
1249 Arch Bracket, p.117

1310n12 12" - 3 Spool Fan Bracket, pp.105, 112
1310n15 15" - 3 Spool Fan Bracket, p.97
1311 17-1/2" - 4 Spool Fan Bracket, p.116
1312 9-1/2" - 3 Ball Fan Bracket, p.95
1314 9-1/2" - 4 Spool Fan Bracket, p.98
1329 28 Ball Fan Bracket, p.152
1330 11" - 12 Ball Fan Bracket, pp.136, 154
1384 13-3/4" - 12 Ball Fan Bracket, p.151
1385 11" - 8 Ball Fan Bracket, p.155

1551 Little Belt Course, p.99
1553 Fancy Belt Course, pp.83 and many others

161-015 Traditional Baluster 2"x18", p.99
161-020 Traditional Baluster 2"x24", pp.87, 92-94, 160
161-040 Traditional Baluster 3"x18", pp.118, 120
161-045 Traditional Baluster 3"x24", pp.89, and many others
161-050 Traditional Baluster 3"x28", p.98
161-070 Heritage Baluster, 3"x32", p.129

201-005 S Rail, p.99
201-135 P2 Rail, pp.83, and many others
201-170 P3 Rail, pp.89, and many others

4132 6-1/2" Wistaria Spandrel, pp.87, 105, 118, 120
4133 8-1/2" Wistaria Spandrel, pp.124-125, 128
4135 Willow Spandrel, p.113
4136 Dogwood Spandrel, p.154
4137 11" Ball & Dowel Spandrel, pp.106, 112
4139 11" Fan Spandrel, p.153
4140 13-3/4" Fan Spandrel, p.150
4141 17-3/4" Fan Spandrel, p.127
4144 3-1/2" Ball & Dowel Spandrel, p.160
4145 9-1/2" Spindle Spandrel, pp.132, 137
4146 9-3/4" Traditional Spandrel, p.89
4147 11-1/4" Traditional Spandrel, p.98
4148 14-1/4" Traditional Spandrel, pp.99, 113
4150 11-3/4" Plain Spool Spandrel, pp.116, 120, 135
4151 SB#5 Spandrel, pp.140-142

5201 2"x2" Drop, pp.104, 123
5201n5 2"x2" Drop (5-3/4" long), p.143
5203 1-1/2"x2" Extender, pp.102, 143
5206 1-1/2"x1-1/2" Extender, p.121
5207n5 1-1/2"x1-1/2" Drop (5-3/4" long), p.121

56-010 SR2 Subrail, pp.83, and many others
56-020 SR3 Subrail, pp.89, and many others

5605 Sloped-top Bottom Rail, pp.83, and many others
5610 Beaded Rail, 1-1/2"x2-1/2", pp.105, and many others

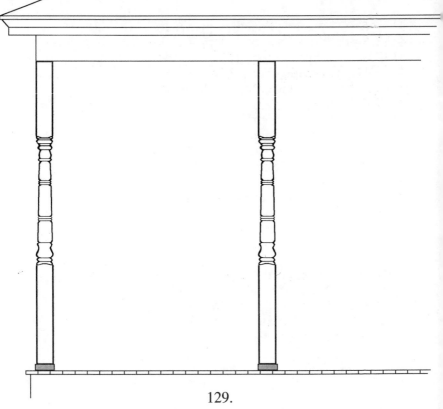

129.

Our first example is the *basic* porch upon which most of our remaining examples are based. The *bottom* width of the eave overhang (the *soffit*) is 8 inches. The Beam is also 8 inches high. Unless otherwise noted, these two dimensions will be standard for the remainder of our porch examples.

The Porch Posts are positioned approximately 6 feet *on center*, (center of one to center of next) and are set *flush* with the front of the Beam (in fact, the Beam is the same 5-1/4" wide as the Posts). This arrangement permits easy installation of Post Face Brackets. We will always show our Porch Posts installed with Base Blocks, which are available in redwood to fit each size of Post. These (or Base Mounting Plates) should always be used to protect the Post *bottoms* from moisture.

For each porch example in this Chapter, we will list the *decorative items* used, giving the Vintage Wood Works item number and description, as follows:

Posts #121-065. Traditional 6"x96", with 32"base, 6' on center.

100.

This is the *same* porch as our first example, but we've added some "Gingerbread", including the very important Third Dimension items (Post Face & Belt Course Brackets in this example).

Post #121-065. Traditional 6"x96", with 32" base, 6' on center.
Post Face Bracket #1131. 23" Cupid's Key, 1-1/2" thick.
Belt Course Bracket #1553. Fancy Belt Course, 12" on center.
Bracket # 1118. Circle Crescent Bracket, framed.
Sawn Baluster #2316. Spear Baluster, spaced together.
Handrail #201-135. P-2 Rail, with SR2 Subrail #56-010.
Bottom Rail #5605. Sloped-top Bottom Rail, shown with
  center support block.

120.

For comparison, here's porch #100 *without* a Beam, and thus no place for Belt Course Brackets. The entire porch appears less balanced. In real life this will be even more noticeable, and the Flying Circle Brackets will tend to be lost in the shadow of the eave. We do still have Post Face Brackets, and they will go a long way to give this porch a three dimensional feel.

As we pointed out earlier, you should try to find older homes in your area that *do* have Post Face and Belt Course Brackets, so you can study their impact. Please also study our next example, to discover you *can* have a Beam even when you don't!

Post #121-065. Traditional 6"x96", with 32" base, 6' on center.
Post Face Bracket #1131. 23" Cupid's Key, 1-1/2" thick.
Bracket # 1114. Flying Circle Bracket, unframed.
Sawn Baluster #2316. Spear Baluster, spaced together.
Handrail #201-135. P-2 Rail, with SR2 Subrail #56-010.
Bottom Rail #5605. Sloped-top Bottom Rail.

143.

And here's a repeat of #120, still *without* a Beam. But we've given the *illusion* of a beam by the use of 2x10 boards *between* each pair of Posts! Notice the Post *tops* go all the way to the eave. Our Flying Circle Brackets are back out of the shadows again, and there's now a place for Belt Course Brackets (installed directly onto the 2x10). This "false beam" approach is great for existing porches built *without* exposed beams, or for porches where height to the eave is not sufficient for a true beam *above* the Posts. See also porch #145, page 88, where we "added to" a short Beam.

Post #121-065. Traditional 6"x96", with 32" base, 6' on center.
Post Face Bracket #1131. 23" Cupid's Key, 1-1/2" thick.
Belt Course Bracket #1553. Fancy Belt Course, 12" on center.
Bracket # 1114. Flying Circle Bracket, unframed.
Sawn Baluster #2316. Spear Baluster, spaced 3" apart.
Handrail #201-135. P-2 Rail, with SR2 Subrail #56-010.
Bottom Rail #5605. Sloped-top Bottom Rail.

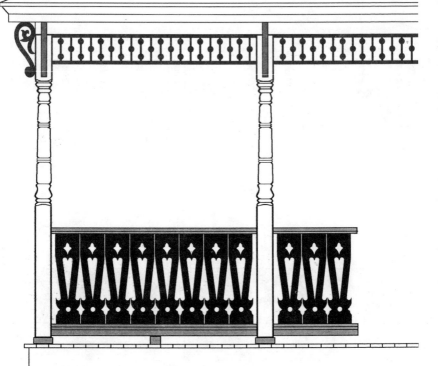

122.

Continuing our study of beams, this example is only 4" high. While that's sufficient Beam to get our Gingerbread (a Spandrel in this case) somewhat out of the eave shadow, it limits our choice of Belt Course Brackets. Still, it's much better than no Beam!

Notice also that the Porch Post has changed to a 42" base, with only a 14" top. This is a common problem with modern existing porches. There's really no room for a Bracket below our Spandrel, should we want one.

Post #121-062. Traditional 6"x96", with 42" base, 6' on center.
Post Face Bracket #1121. Bird of Paradise, 1-1/2" thick, unframed.
Spandrel #4117. 8-3/4" Ball & Dowel Spandrel.
Sawn Baluster #2320. Heart & Fleur Baluster, spaced together.
Handrail #201-135. P-2 Rail, with SR2 Subrail #56-010.
Bottom Rail #5605. Sloped-top Bottom Rail.

125.

Here's #122 improved, despite short Beam & Post top. Belt Course Brackets are *1-1/2" thick* Little Swan Brackets, un-framed, used horizontally. Spandrels *between* pairs of SR#4 Brackets maximize available Post top. (Spandrels 7" or less in height fit the SR#4.)

Posts look nicer with turned portions lower, but we're working with what we found on this porch. We've resisted moving the Handrail higher, as this would only highlight the problem.

Post #121-062. Traditional 6"x96", with 42" base, 6' on center.
Post Face Bracket #1121. Bird of Paradise, 1-1/2" thick, unframed.
Belt Course Bracket #1108. Little Swan, 12" o.c., 1-1/2" thick, unframed.
Bracket # 1174. SR#4 Bracket, with Drop attached.
Spandrel #4132. 6-1/2" Wistaria Spandrel.
Baluster #161-020. Traditional Baluster, 2"x24", 6" on center.
Handrail #201-135. P-2 Rail, with SR2 Subrail #56-010.
Bottom Rail #5605. Sloped-top Bottom Rail.

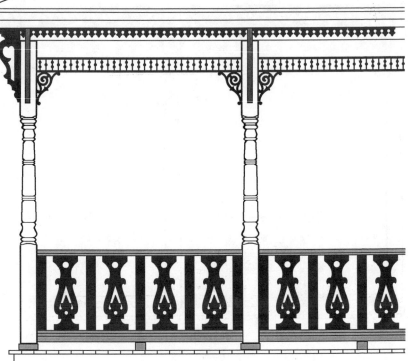

145.

Here's #122 one last time, still with 4" high Beam, but with more appropriate Posts. Their 24" tops provide these benefits:
- Space for a false beam (2x8's) between pairs of Posts.
- Space for a longer Post Face Bracket.
- Less flat Post base above the Handrail.
- A more pleasing balance to the entire porch.

Post #121-065. Traditional 6"x96", with 32" base, 6' on center.
Post Face Bracket #1131. 23" Cupid's Key, 1-1/2"thick.
Applique #2206n3. Fleur Running Trim, 3-3/8" size.
Spandrel #4106. 4-1/2" Ball & Dowel Spandrel.
Bracket #1231. FB#1, unframed.
Sawn Baluster #2316. Spear Baluster, 8" on center.
Handrail #201-135. P-2 Rail, with SR2 Subrail #56-010.
Bottom Rail #5605. Sloped-top Bottom Rail, shown with
  center support block.

121.

Although not as common, you may have a porch with an extra
deep Beam, such as the 12" height shown here. This is great,
and affords a wide range of possibilities. Here we show a larger Running Trim used as an applique against the Beam. It could
also be suspended from the *forward edge* of the eave, providing an icicle or drapery effect, while leaving room for Belt
Course Brackets on the Beam.

Post #121-065. Traditional 6"x96", with 32" base, 6' on center.
Post Face Bracket #1130. 36" Cupid's Key, 1-1/2" thick.
Applique #2206n7. Fleur Running Trim, 7" size.
Spandrel #4146. 9-3/4" Traditional Spandrel.
Bracket #1242. FB#6 Bracket, unframed, horizontal position.
Baluster #161-045. Traditional Baluster, 3"x24", 6" on center.
Handrail #201-070. P-3 Rail, with SR3 Subrail #56-020.
Bottom Rail #5605. Sloped-top Bottom Rail, shown with
  center support.

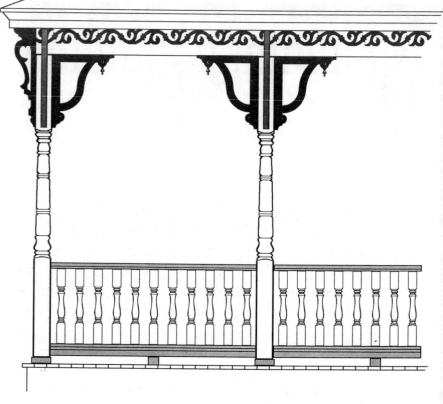

111.

We're back to our "standard" 8" Beam height. We'll explore, in the next several illustrations, additional decorative techniques for the Beam area. This and the facing page show two positions for an Applique installed directly onto the face of the Beam.

Post #121-065. Traditional 6"x96", with 32" base, 6' on center.
Post Face Bracket #1132. 31" Cupid's Key, 1-1/2" thick.
Applique #2209n5. Wistaria Running Trim, 5" size.
Bracket # 1115. Dove's Wing, 1-1/2" thick.
Baluster #161-045. Traditional Baluster, 3"x24", 6" on center.
Handrail #201-070. P-3 Rail, with SR3 Subrail #56-020.
Bottom Rail #5605. Sloped-top Bottom Rail, shown with
  center support block.

112.

Same porch, but with the Applique *centered* on the Beam. (And we've also changed *Brackets*, but I'm sure your trained eye noticed that immediately!)

Post #121-065. Traditional 6"x96", with 32" base, 6' on center.
Post Face Bracket #1132. 31" Cupid's Key, 1-1/2" thick.
Applique #2209n5. Wistaria Running Trim, 5" size.
Bracket # 1105. Cupid's Arrow Bracket, 1-1/2" thick.
Baluster #161-045. Traditional Baluster, 3"x24", 6" on center.
Handrail #201-070. P-3 Rail, with SR3 Subrail #56-020.
Bottom Rail #5605. Sloped-top Bottom Rail, shown with
  center support block.

106.

These two pages also show Running Trim as Applique, but the facing page additionally illustrates the use of Running Trim *between* Belt Course Brackets.

Here we've used a smaller 10" (12" including frame) size of our Footed Crescent Bracket. However, the next larger size (#1111n15) would strengthen the "archway" effect these curved Brackets provide. Turn back to the preceding page and notice the increased effectiveness the larger Cupid's Arrow Brackets gave to porch #112.

Post #121-065. Traditional 6"x96", with 32" base, 6' on center.
Post Face Bracket #1132. 31" Cupid's Key, 1-1/2" thick.
Applique #2225n3. Arrowhead Running Trim, 3-3/8" size.
Bracket # 1111n10. Footed Crescent, 10" size, framed.
Baluster #161-020. Traditional Baluster, 2"x24", 6" on center.
Handrail #201-135. P-2 Rail, with SR2 Subrail #56-010.
Bottom Rail #5605. Sloped-top Bottom Rail, shown with
  center support block.

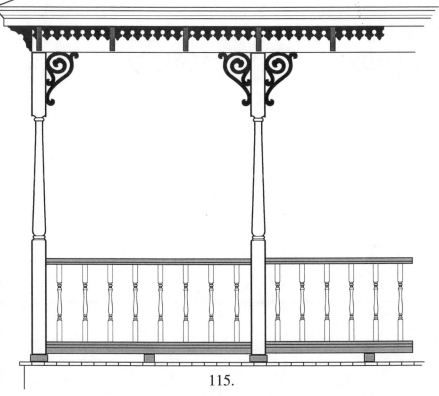

115.

Running Trim works well *between* Belt Course Brackets. Also, we've omitted the Post Face Brackets for this example. While the Belt Course Brackets work well, we feel it would be a more attractive porch *with* Post Face Brackets. However, we want you to see these differences for yourself.

Notice also that the Posts are a plainer style (and thinner), the Balusters are more widely spaced, and there's no Spandrel. Thus, we have a rather simple, understated porch.

Post #121-100. New Orleans 5"x96", with 36" base, 6' o.c.
Belt Course Bracket #1553. Fancy Belt Course, 24" o.c.
Applique #2206n5. Fleur Running Trim, 5" size.
Bracket #1119. 17" Scroll Bracket, unframed.
Baluster #161-020. Traditional Baluster, 2"x24", 8" on center.
Handrail #201-135. P-2 Rail, with SR2 Subrail #56-010.
Bottom Rail #5605. Sloped-top Bottom Rail, shown with
   center support block.

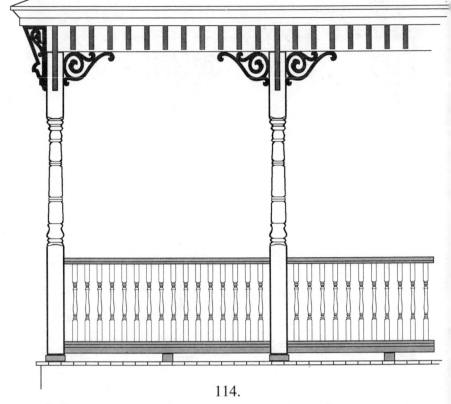

114.

These two pages illustrate more *tightly* spaced Belt Course Brackets. This example also allows a good comparison with several items from the previous page (example #115). We've turned the 17" Scroll Brackets horizontally, added Post Face Brackets, spaced Balusters more tightly, and increased Posts to the 6" size. Please note the more substantial effect these subtle changes provide to a porch that is still rather simple in overall design.

Post #121-060. Traditional 6"x96", with 36" base, 6' on center.
Post Face Bracket #1113. Swan's Neck, 1-1/2" thick, unframed.
Belt Course Bracket #1553. Fancy Belt Course, 6" on center.
Bracket #1119. 17" Scroll Bracket, unframed, horizontal.
Baluster #161-020. Traditional Baluster, 2"x24", 4" on center.
Handrail #201-135. P-2 Rail, with SR2 Subrail #56-010.
Bottom Rail #5605. Sloped-top Bottom Rail, shown with center support block.

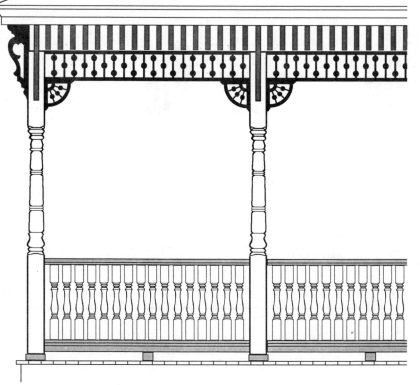

124.

Perhaps the spacing here is *too* close on both the Belt Course Brackets and the Balusters, but our goal is to provide a very wide range of possibilities for your review. The tight spacing here may work for very small porches. Close Belt Course Brackets *do* work well at the eave of a two-story tower or turret, should you be lucky enough to have one!

Post #121-065. Traditional 6"x96", with 32" base, 6' on center.
Post Face Bracket #1131. 23" Cupid's Key, 1-1/2" thick.
Belt Course Bracket #1553. Fancy Belt Course, 4" on center.
Spandrel #4117. 8-3/4" Ball & Dowel Spandrel.
Bracket # 1312. 9-1/2" - 3 Ball Fan Bracket.
Baluster #161-045. Traditional Baluster, 3"x24", 4" on center.
Handrail #201-070. P-3 Rail, with SR3 Subrail #56-020.
Bottom Rail #5605. Sloped-top Bottom Rail, shown with
   center support block.

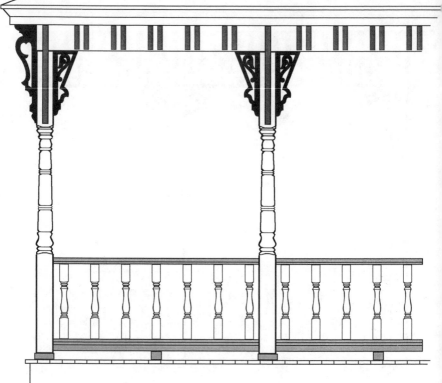

105.

Belt Course Brackets in *pairs* are very traditional. These are set 12" from the center of one pair to the center of the next. Likewise, it's 12" from the center of the Post Face Bracket to the center of the first pair of Belt Course Brackets, but this distance could be less.

At 10" on center, the Balusters are further apart than we prefer. If this was done for budget reasons, consider using the 2" size, spaced more closely. Or (if safety is not a factor), since the 3" size Balusters are so nice, just wait until later to add the balustrade. It'll make a totally unique Christmas present!

Post #121-065. Traditional 6"x96", with 32" base, 6' on center.
Post Face Bracket #1132. 31" Cupid's Key, 1-1/2" thick.
Belt Course Bracket #1553. Fancy Belt Course, pairs, 12" o.c.
Bracket # 1113. Swan's Neck Bracket, unframed.
Baluster #161-045. Traditional Baluster, 3"x24", 10" o.c.
Handrail #201-070. P-3 Rail, with SR3 Subrail #56-020.
Bottom Rail #5605. Sloped-top Bottom Rail.

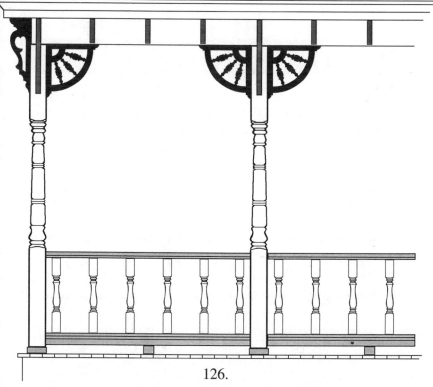

126.

More widely spaced Belt Course Brackets are also an option. These are 18" on center. Wider than about 24" o.c. (next example), they begin to loose a lot of their charm...

Here we're even further apart (12" o.c.) on our Balusters, and they're just *not* very appealing.

Post #121-065. Traditional 6"x96", with 32" base, 6' on center.
Post Face Bracket #1131. 23" Cupid's Key, 1-1/2" thick.
Belt Course Bracket #1553. Fancy Belt Course 18" o.c.
Bracket # 1310n15. 15" - 3 Spool Fan Bracket.
Baluster #161-045. Traditional Baluster, 3"x24", 12" o.c.
Handrail #201-070. P-3 Rail, with SR3 Subrail #56-020.
Bottom Rail #5605. Sloped-top Bottom Rail, shown with
  center support block.

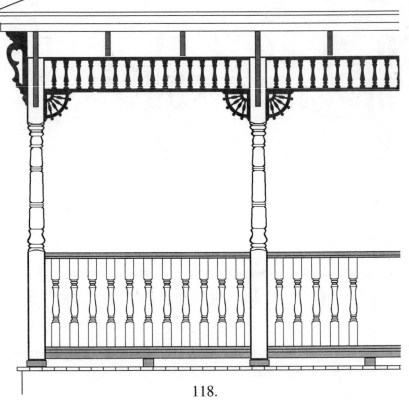

118.

These two porches offer some interesting comparisons. This example uses a taller 28" Baluster (36" to top of Handrail), but since they're spaced 6" o.c., it works very well. Post top is only 20" long (since we've gone with a 36" base), but everything looks very nice. Tighter spacing of Belt Course Brackets would give even more balance to the entire effect.

Post #121-060. Traditional 6"x96", with 36" base, 6' on center.
Post Face Bracket #1131. 23" Cupid's Key, 1-1/2" thick.
Belt Course Bracket #1553. Fancy Belt Course, 24" o.c.
Spandrel #4147. 11-1/4" Traditional Spandrel.
Bracket #1314. 9-1/2" - 4 Spool Fan Bracket.
Baluster #161-050. Traditional Baluster, 3"x28", 6" on center.
Handrail #201-070. P-3 Rail, with SR3 Subrail #56-020.
Bottom Rail #5605. Sloped-top Bottom Rail, shown with
  center support block.

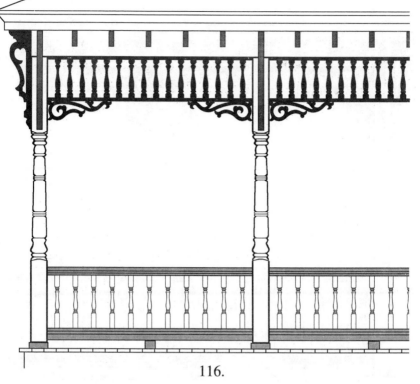

116.

In contrast, this porch has very short Balusters (24" Handrail height, and Posts were trimmed to 27" bases). Spandrel is taller, and Belt Course Brackets are closer. Emphasis is now at the *top* of the porch.

Please study these two examples closely. We've preached for many years that modern porches' Handrails are too high. Short Balusters are very traditional, unless safety or code requirements are a factor, such as on a second story porch.

Post #121-065. Traditional 6"x96", with 27" base, 6' on center, modified.
Post Face Bracket #1132. 31" Cupid's Key, 1-1/2" thick.
Belt Course Bracket #1551. Little Belt Course, 12" o.c.
Bracket # 1103. 21" Scroll Bracket, unframed, horizontal.
Spandrel #4148. 14-1/4" Traditional Spandrel.
Baluster #161-015. Traditional Baluster, 2"x18", 6" on center.
Handrail #201-005. S Rail, with SR2 Subrail #56-010.
Bottom Rail #5605. Sloped-top Bottom Rail.

107.

Here we find two very pleasing porches. The effect is substantial, and is achieved with a minimum number of items. Three inch thick Corbels as a belt course... full length Post Face Brackets... larger (and 1-1/2" thick) Brackets... and our favorite (6" on center) spacing of turned Balusters ... all lend an air of elegant permanence.

Post #121-065. Traditional 6"x96", with 32" base, 6' on center.
Post Face Bracket #1132. 31" Cupid's Key, 1-1/2" thick.
Corbel #301s (as belt course). Classic Corbel, horizontal,
   10" on center.
Bracket # 1117. Andover Bracket, 1-1/2" thick.
Baluster #161-045. Traditional Baluster, 3"x24", 6" on center.
Handrail #201-070. P-3 Rail, with SR3 Subrail #56-020.
Bottom Rail #5605. Sloped-top Bottom Rail, shown with
   center support block.

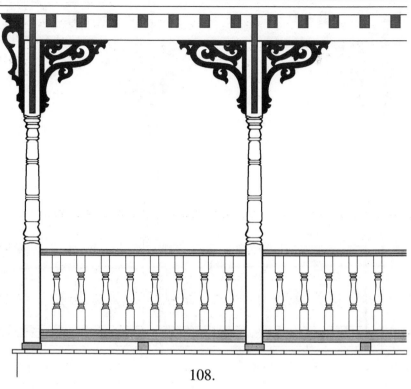

108.

Almost the same porch, but turning the Brackets horizontally and separating the Balusters *has* made a difference. Which one do you prefer?

Post #121-065. Traditional 6"x96", with 32" base, 6' on center.
Post Face Bracket #1132. 31" Cupid's Key, 1-1/2" thick.
Corbel #301s (as belt course). Classic Corbel, horizontal, 10" on center.
Bracket # 1117. Andover Bracket, 1-1/2" thick, horizontal.
Baluster #161-045. Traditional Baluster, 3"x24", 8" on center.
Handrail #201-070. P-3 Rail, with SR3 Subrail #56-020.
Bottom Rail #5605. Sloped-top Bottom Rail, shown with center support block.

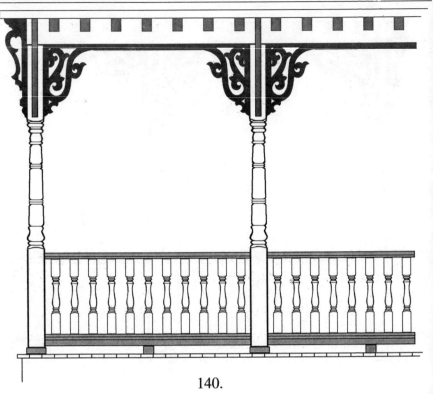

140.

These two pages continue with the Andover Bracket. Here the ends of the Brackets were blunt cut before installation, and our Extender was fitted between each pair of Brackets.

Post #121-065. Traditional 6"x96", with 32" base, 6' on center.
Post Face Bracket #1132. 31" Cupid's Key, 1-1/2" thick.
Corbel #301S (as belt course). Classic Corbel, horizontal,
   10" on center.
Bracket # 1117. Andover Bracket, 1-1/2" thick, modified.
Extender #5203. 1-1/2"x2".
Baluster #161-045. Traditional Baluster, 3"x24", 6" on center.
Handrail #201-070. P-3 Rail, with SR3 Subrail #56-020.
Bottom Rail #5605. Sloped-top Bottom Rail, shown with
   center support block.

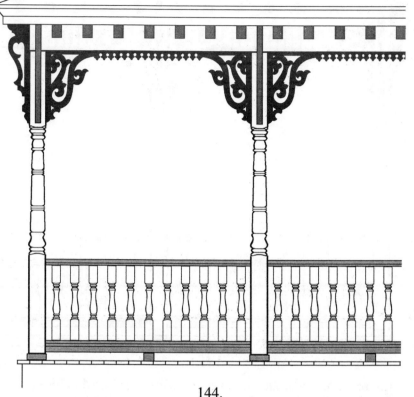

144.

Again the ends of the Andover Brackets were blunt cut before installation, but this time Running Trim was installed between pairs of Brackets.

Post #121-065. Traditional 6"x96", with 32" base, 6' on center.
Post Face Bracket #1132. 31" Cupid's Key, 1-1/2" thick.
Corbel #301S (as belt course). Classic Corbel, horizontal, 10" on center.
Bracket # 1117. Andover Bracket, 1-1/2" thick, modified.
Running Trim #2206n3. Fleur Running Trim, 3-3/8" size.
Baluster #161-045. Traditional Baluster, 3"x24", 6" on center.
Handrail #201-070. P-3 Rail, with SR3 Subrail #56-020.
Bottom Rail #5605. Sloped-top Bottom Rail, shown with center support block.

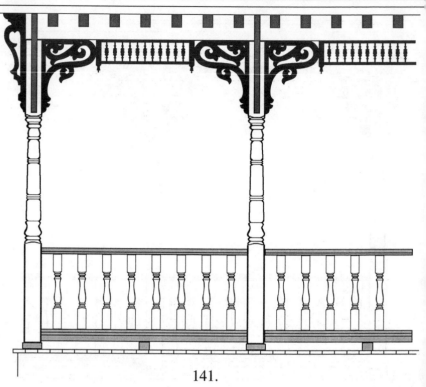

141.

And one final time the Andover Brackets are altered before installation. By placing Drops *beside* these modified Andovers, we were able to use a Spandrel between each pair of Brackets. The effect is very nice...

Post #121-065. Traditional 6"x96", with 32" base, 6' on center.
Post Face Bracket #1132. 31" Cupid's Key, 1-1/2" thick.
Corbel #301S (as belt course). Classic Corbel, horizontal, 10" on center.
Spandrel #4127. 7" Spool Spandrel.
Drop #5201. 2"x2" Drop, 10-3/4" long.
Bracket # 1117. Andover Bracket, 1-1/2" thick, modified.
Baluster #161-045. Traditional Baluster, 3"x24", 8" on center.
Handrail #201-070. P-3 Rail, with SR3 Subrail #56-020.
Bottom Rail #5605. Sloped-top Bottom Rail, shown with center support block.

139.

The use of larger Corbels as a belt course is also possible, although for this somewhat dainty Spandrel, the *smaller* Classic Corbel might be a safer choice.

We've used a Beaded Rail under the Spandrel. This is very traditional... common in the past century... and should be used more on present day porches. It's a very effective way to blend the various decorative components.

Post #121-065. Traditional 6"x96", with 32" base, 6' on center.
Post Face Bracket #1132. 31" Cupid's Key, 1-1/2" thick.
Corbel #301 (as belt course). Classic Corbel, 12" on center.
Spandrel #4132. 6-1/2" Wistaria Spandrel.
Beaded Rail #5610. 1-1/2" x 2-1/2".
Bracket # 1310n12. 12" - 3 Spool Fan Bracket.
Baluster #161-045. Traditional Baluster, 3"x24", 6" on center.
Handrail #201-070. P-3 Rail, with SR3 Subrail #56-020.
Bottom Rail #5605. Sloped-top Bottom Rail, shown with
   center support block.

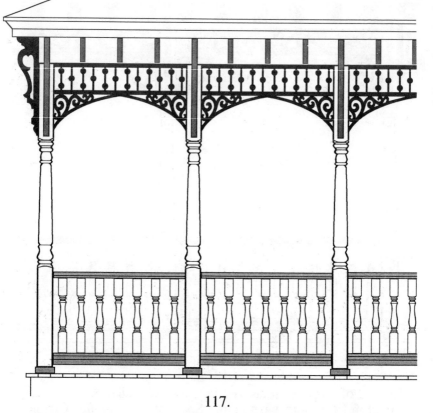

117.

On this and the next few pages we'll vary the Post *spacing*. Most of the examples in this Chapter have Posts that are 6 feet on center, but here we find a very tight 4 feet from center to center. Before you try this in "real life", you may want to nail some scrap lumber up to represent Posts, and experiment with different spacings on your actual porch.

Post #121-075. Classic 5"x96", with 32" base, 4' on center.
Post Face Bracket #1132. 31" Cupid's Key, 1-1/2" thick.
Belt Course Bracket #1553. Fancy Belt Course, 12" o.c.
Spandrel #4117. 8-3/4" Ball & Dowel Spandrel.
Bracket # 1247. The Arch Bracket, shortened, unframed.
Baluster #161-045. Traditional Baluster, 3"x24", 6" on center.
Handrail #201-070. P-3 Rail, with SR3 Subrail #56-020.
Bottom Rail #5605. Sloped-top Bottom Rail, shown with
   center support block.

146.

Here's the same basic porch, but with Posts spaced 5 feet on center.

Post #121-075. Classic 5"x96", with 32" base, 5' on center.
Post Face Bracket #1132. 31" Cupid's Key, 1-1/2" thick.
Belt Course Bracket #1553. Fancy Belt Course, 12" o.c.
Spandrel #4120. 7" Ball & Dowel Spandrel.
Bracket # 1235n12. F.B.#4 Bracket, framed.
Baluster #161-045. Traditional Baluster, 3"x24", 6" on center.
Handrail #201-070. P-3 Rail, with SR3 Subrail #56-020.
Bottom Rail #5605. Sloped-top Bottom Rail, shown with
  center support block.

119.

In contrast, now we're at 8 foot on center spacing with our Posts. This example looks too sparse. Its widely spaced Balusters and minimal decoration at the top of the porch accentuate the wider distance between Posts.

Post #121-084. Classic 6"x96", with 32" base, 8' on center.
Bracket #1232n11. F.B.#2 Bracket, unframed.
Sawn Baluster #2316. Spear Baluster, 16" on center.
Handrail #201-135. P-2 Rail, with SR2 Subrail #56-010.
Bottom Rail #5605. Sloped-top Bottom Rail, shown with
    center support block.

142.

But as we see here, 8 foot Post spacing *will* easily work. We just needed more Gingerbread to balance things!

Post #121-084. Classic 6"x96", with 32" base, 8' on center.
Post Face Bracket #1132. 31" Cupid's Key, 1-1/2" thick.
Belt Course Bracket #1553. Fancy Belt Course, 12" o.c.
Spandrel #4103. 6" Ball & Dowel Spandrel.
Bracket # 1232n11. F.B.#2 Bracket, unframed.
Sawn Baluster #2316. Spear Baluster, 11" on center.
Handrail #201-135. P-2 Rail, with SR2 Subrail #56-010.
Bottom Rail #5605. Sloped-top Bottom Rail.

130.

Posts can be used in *pairs* when a somewhat heavier look is desired. This may be a good solution when you need quite a bit of space *between* Posts (to avoid a window, for example), but don't want the Posts to look "skimpy". In this example our four Posts occupy about 7'8" overall, with 4" clear between each pair.

Post #121-065. Traditional 6"x96", with 32" base.
Post Face Bracket #1131. 23" Cupid's Key, 1-1/2" thick.
Belt Course Bracket #1553. Fancy Belt Course, 10" o.c.
Spandrel #4128. 10" Spool Spandrel.
Bracket # 1102. Parrot's Beak Bracket, unframed.
Baluster #161-045. Traditional Baluster, 3"x24", 6" on center.
Handrail #201-070. P-3 Rail, with SR3 Subrail #56-020.
Bottom Rail #5605. Sloped-top Bottom Rail, shown with
  center support block.

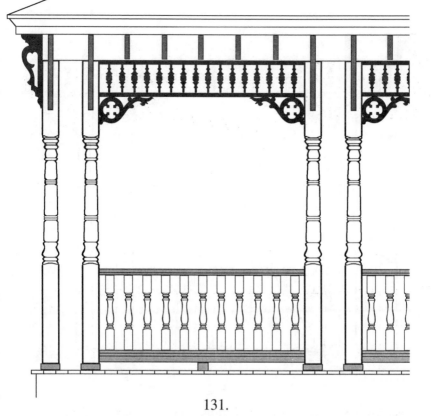

131.

Now we have 8" clear between each pair of Posts. Together the four Posts occupy about 8'4". Compare this with porch #132 on the following page...

Post #121-065. Traditional 6"x96", with 32" base.
Post Face Bracket #1131. 23" Cupid's Key, 1-1/2" thick.
Belt Course Bracket #1553. Fancy Belt Course, 12" o.c.
Spandrel #4129. 11-3/4" Spool Spandrel.
Bracket # 1107. Gothic Circle Bracket, unframed, horizontal.
Baluster #161-045. Traditional Baluster, 3"x24", 6" on center.
Handrail #201-070. P-3 Rail, with SR3 Subrail #56-020.
Bottom Rail #5605. Sloped-top Bottom Rail.

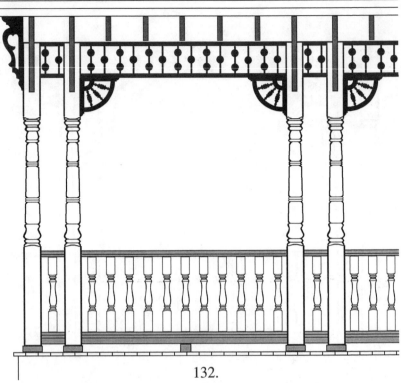

132.

We're repeating the prior example (#131), but with Balustrade and Spandrels *between* the pairs of Posts. Unless your space between pairs is *less* than about 5", you will probably want Balustrade between each pair of Posts.

Post #121-065. Traditional 6"x96", with 32" base, 8" clear
   between pairs of Post.
Post Face Bracket #1131. 23" Cupid's Key, 1-1/2" thick.
Belt Course Bracket #1553. Fancy Belt Course, 12" o.c.
Spandrel #4137. 11" Ball & Dowel Spandrel.
Bracket # 1310n12. 12" - 3 Spool Fan Bracket.
Baluster #161-045. Traditional Baluster, 3"x24", 6" on center.
Handrail #201-070. P-3 Rail, with SR3 Subrail #56-020.
Bottom Rail #5605. Sloped-top Bottom Rail, shown with
   center support block.

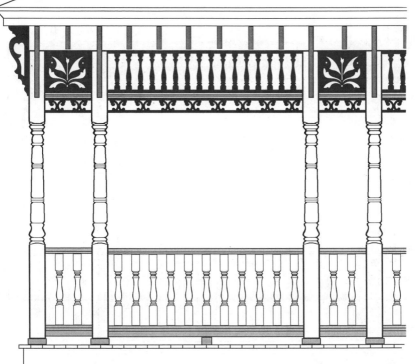

133.

And here we find *two* Balusters between each pair of Posts. In this example the four Posts occupy about 9'8" overall, with 16-1/2" clear between each pair. This allows room to position The Tulip Medallion in this space. By using Beaded Rail below our Medallions and Traditional Spandrels, we've created horizontal definition that ties the entire porch together, while nicely setting off the Willow Spandrels installed below.

Post #121-065. Traditional 6"x96", with 32" base, 16-1/2" clear between pairs of Posts.
Post Face Bracket #1131. 23" Cupid's Key, 1-1/2" thick.
Belt Course Bracket #1553. Fancy Belt Course, 10" o.c.
Medallion #2505. Tulip Medallion.
Spandrel #4148. 14-1/4" Traditional Spandrel.
Spandrel #4135. Willow Spandrel.
Beaded Rail #5610. 1-1/2"x2-1/2".
Baluster #161-045. Traditional Baluster, 3"x24", 6" on center.
Handrail #201-070. P-3 Rail, with SR3 Subrail #56-020.
Bottom Rail #5605. Sloped-top Bottom Rail.

138.

With 18-3/4" between each pair of Posts, we can use The Shell
Fretwork Panel. The four Posts occupy about 10' overall.
Beaded Rail below The Shell would work well here, as it does
on the preceding example. But, as always, we want to illustrate
a wide variety of possibilities.

Post #121-065. Traditional 6"x96", with 32" base, 18-3/4"
   clear between pairs of Posts.
Post Face Bracket #1131. 23" Cupid's Key 1-1/2" thick.
Belt Course Bracket #1553. Fancy Belt Course, 12" o.c.
Medallion #2511n18. The Shell, 18-3/4" size.
Spandrel #4128. 10" Spool Spandrel.
Bracket #1233. F.B.#3 Bracket, unframed.
Baluster #161-045. Traditional Baluster, 3"x24", 6" on center.
Handrail #201-070. P-3 Rail, with SR3 Subrail #56-020.
Bottom Rail #5605. Sloped-top Bottom Rail.

127.

The Victoria Circle Medallion is a strong contender for use between pairs of Posts! Turned *horizontally*, as shown, it is a perfect fit for The Eloise, The Lisa, or the 13-3/4" Fan Spandrels. We can also frame this Medallion to be used *vertically*, where it is a perfect match for the The Lily Langtry or 17-3/4" Fan Spandrels.

Post #121-065. Traditional 6"x96", with 32" base, 17-3/4" clear between pairs of Posts.
Post Face Bracket #1131. 23" Cupid's Key, 1-1/2" thick.
Applique #2225n3. Arrowhead Running Trim, 3-3/8" size.
Medallion #2502. Victoria Circle Medallion.
Spandrel #4105. Eloise Spandrel.
Baluster #161-045. Traditional Baluster, 3"x24", uneven spacing... looks "tacky" once noticed!
Handrail #201-070. P-3 Rail, with SR3 Subrail #56-020.
Bottom Rail #5605. Sloped-top Bottom Rail.

113.

These 9' tall Posts were cut on the job from 10' Posts. Please notice that the extra foot was removed entirely from the *bottom* of the Posts, leaving the 31" long top portion available for generously sized Spandrel and Fan Brackets. This also left a 37" tall Post base, providing a comfortable fit for the 36" high Handrail of this example.

Post #121-055. Traditional 6"x120", 6' on center, *modified.*
Post Face Bracket #1130. 36" Cupid's Key, 1-1/2" thick.
Belt Course Bracket #1553. Fancy Belt Course, 12" o.c.
Spandrel #4150. 11-3/4" Plain Spool Spandrel.
Bracket #1311. 17-1/2" - 4" Spool Fan Bracket.
Sawn Baluster #2320. Heart & Fleur Baluster, spaced together.
Handrail #201-135. P-2 Rail, with SR2 Subrail #56-010.
Bottom Rail #5605. Sloped-top Bottom Rail.

147.

The *base* portion is very tall on these full 10' Post. Our 45-1/2"
high Handrail may be awkward in "real life". Avoid Posts over
about 9' tall by using deeper Beams, etc., and always remove
excess only from 10' Posts' *base* area.

Post #121-055. Traditional 6"x120", with 49" base, 6' o.c.
Post Face Bracket #1130. 36" Cupid's Key, 1-1/2" thick.
Belt Course Bracket #1553. Fancy Belt Course, 12" o.c.
Spandrel #4130. 16" Ball & Dowel Spandrel.
Spandrel #4119. 8" Ball & Dowel Spandrel, above Balusters.
Bracket # 1249. Arch Bracket, unframed.
Beaded Rail #5610. 1-1/2"x2-1/2".
Sawn Baluster #2320. Heart & Fleur Baluster, spaced together.
Handrail #201-135. P-2 Rail, with SR2 Subrail #56-010.
Bottom Rail #5605. Sloped-top Bottom Rail.

110.

These two porches use the SR#4 Bracket we first saw on page 87 (illustration #125). In this example, the Post Face Brackets extend well beyond the bottoms of the SR#4 Brackets, while the adjoining porch's Post Face Brackets end just below the SR#4. Either is fine. Which do you prefer?

Post #121-065. Traditional 6"x96", with 32" base, 6' on center.
Post Face Bracket #1132. 31" Cupid's Key, 1-1/2" thick.
Belt Course Bracket #1553. Fancy Belt Course, 12" o.c.
Spandrel #4132. 6-1/2" Wistaria Spandrel (also used below
    P3 rail).
Bracket #1174. SR #4 Bracket (drop attached).
Beaded Rail #5610. 1-1/2" x 2-1/2".
Baluster #161-040. Traditional Baluster, 3"x18", 6" on center.
Handrail #201-070. P-3 Rail, with SR3 Subrail #56-020.
Bottom Rail #5605. Sloped-top Bottom Rail, shown with
    center support block.

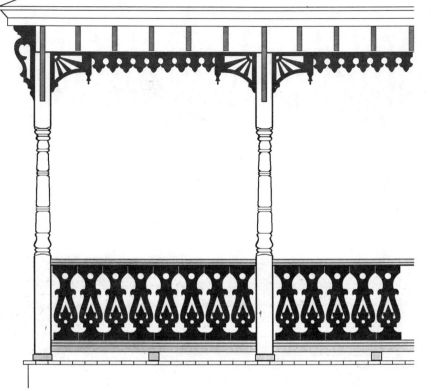

109.

The repeating pattern of sawn Spear Balusters complements the Fleur Running Trim's repetitive design. This would be a good place to use our optional *Top Rail* on the Running Trim (not shown here). That would bring the Fleur Running Trim down 3/4" (into better balance with the SR#4 Brackets), while providing additional texture and shadow line.

Post #121-065. Traditional 6"x96", with 32" base, 6' on center.
Post Face Bracket #1131. 23" Cupid's Key, 1-1/2" thick.
Belt Course Bracket #1553. Fancy Belt Course, 12" o.c.
Bracket #1174. SR #4 Bracket (drop attached).
Running Trim #2206n7. Fleur Running Trim, 7" size.
Sawn Baluster #2316. Spear Baluster, spaced together.
Handrail #201-135. P-2 Rail, with SR2 Subrail #56-010.
Bottom Rail #5605. Sloped-top Bottom Rail, shown with center support block.

104.

This porch skillfully combines a variety of decorative elements. The results speak for themselves! Don't hesitate to try your favorite Bracket horizontally, as we did here. And please notice the extra finish the Beaded Rail provides, as used here between Spandrels and Brackets, and also in the Balustrade.

Post #121-065. Traditional 6"x96", with 32" base, 6' on center.
Post Face Bracket #1132. 31" Cupid's Key, 1-1/2" thick.
Belt Course Bracket #1553. Fancy Belt Course, 12" o.c.
Spandrel #4150. 11-3/4" Plain Spool Spandrel.
Beaded Rail #5610. 1-1/2" x 2-1/2".
Running Trim #2206n3. Fleur Running Trim, 3-3/8" size.
Bracket #1131. 23" Cupids Key, 1-1/2" thick, horizontal.
Spandrel #4132. 6-1/2" Wistaria Spandrel, used above Balusters.
Baluster #161-040. Traditional Baluster, 3"x18", 6" on center.
Handrail #201-070. P-3 Rail, with SR3 Subrail #56-020.
Bottom Rail #5605. Sloped-top Bottom Rail.

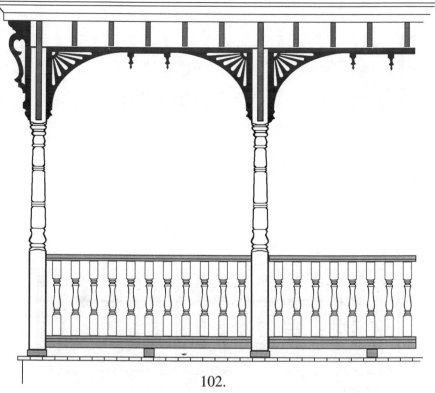

102.

Sun Ray Arch Brackets create dramatic, sweeping arches on any porch. Note that we've used our Extender between Drops to make a smooth transition from one Bracket over to the next.

Post #121-065. Traditional 6"x96", with 32" base, 6' on center.
Post Face Bracket #1132. 31" Cupid's Key, 1-1/2" thick.
Belt Course Bracket #1553. Fancy Belt Course, 12" o.c.
Bracket # 1170n46. Sun Ray Arch Set, trimmed to fit.
Extra drop #5207n5. 1-1/2"x1-1/2" drop.
Extender #5206. 1-1/2" x 1-1/2".
Baluster #161-045. Traditional Baluster, 3"x24", 6" on center.
Handrail #201-070. P-3 Rail, with SR3 Subrail #56-020.
Bottom Rail #5605. Sloped-top Bottom Rail, shown with center support block.

134.

Like the *appeal* of sawn Balusters, but not sure your budget agrees? Center two or three decorative Balusters between each pair of Posts, then fill the remaining Balustrade with straight 1" by 3" "homemade" pickets. Attention is drawn to the fancy work, while the budget survives!

Post #121-065. Traditional 6"x96", with 32" base, 6' on center.
Post Face Bracket #1131. 23" Cupid's Key, 1-1/2" thick.
Belt Course Bracket #1553. Fancy Belt Course, 12" o.c.
Applique #2422. Dogwood Flower Applique.
Bracket # 1121. Bird of Paradise Bracket, unframed.
Sawn Baluster #2316. Spear Baluster, centered.
Handrail #201-135. P-2 Rail, with SR2 Subrail #56-010.
Bottom Rail #5605. Sloped-top Bottom Rail, shown with
  center support block.

148.

Or you can *alternate* Sawn Balusters and plain pickets...
Notice also the use of a Drop piece between Fretwork Spandrels. This allows the use of *two* Spandrels where one would
otherwise be used, thereby increasing the amount of Fretwork
(end and middle pieces).

Post #121-065. Traditional 6"x96", with 32" base, 8' on center.
Post Face Bracket #1131. 23" Cupid's Key, 1-1/2" thick.
Applique # 2225n3. Arrowhead Running Trim, 3-3/8".
Spandrel #4115. Lily Langtry Spandrel.
Drop #5201. 2"x2" Drop.
Sawn Baluster #2305. SB#5 Baluster, trimmed to height.
Handrail #201-135. P-2 Rail, with SR2 Subrail #56-010.
Bottom Rail #5605. Sloped-top Bottom Rail, shown with
   center support block.

123.

This porch is very good, but not great...
These Balusters are perhaps *not* the best choice to complement the very ornate upper decorations. And FB#3 Bracket appears somewhat frail next to the flamboyant Wistaria Spandrel. Let's try again on the adjoining page.

Post #121-065. Traditional 6"x96", with 32" base, 6' on center.
Post Face Bracket #1132. 31" Cupid's Key, 1-1/2" thick.
Belt Course Bracket #1553. Fancy Belt Course, 12" o.c.
Spandrel #4133. 8-1/2" Wistaria Spandrel.
Bracket # 1233. F.B. #3 Bracket, unframed.
Sawn Baluster #2327. Urn Baluster, 12" on center.
Handrail #201-135. P-2 Rail, with SR2 Subrail #56-010.
Bottom Rail #5605. Sloped-top Bottom Rail, shown with
 center support block.

128.

Do you agree this is a more balanced and pleasing porch than example #123? We've substituted the Spear style sawn Balusters, and we've spaced them continuously. And the larger, bolder 17" Scrolls, turned horizontally to fit, and set off with Beaded Rail, hold their own better with this Spandrel. Picky? Perhaps... but if details make the porch, *well chosen* details create a GREAT porch!

Post #121-065. Traditional 6"x96", with 32" base, 6' on center.
Post Face Bracket #1132. 31" Cupid's Key, 1-1/2" thick.
Belt Course Bracket #1553. Fancy Belt Course, 12" o.c.
Spandrel #4133. 8-1/2" Wistaria Spandrel.
Beaded Rail #5610. 1-1/2" x 2-1/2".
Bracket # 1119. 17" Scroll, unframed, horizontal position.
Baluster #2316. Spear Baluster, spaced together.
Handrail #201-135. P-2 Rail, with SR2 Subrail #56-010.
Bottom Rail #5605. Sloped-top Bottom Rail.

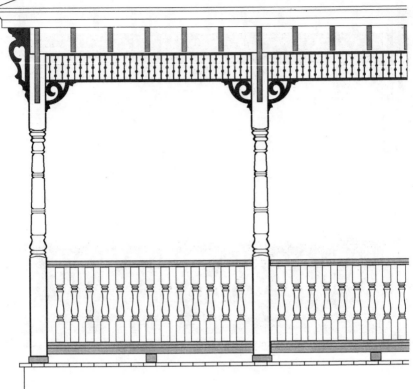

136.

The Balusters are spaced 5" on center here. This is fine (quite preferable to spacing them too far apart), but 6" on center spacing would certainly suffice.

Post #121-065. Traditional 6"x96", with 32" base, 6' on center.
Post Face Bracket #1131. 23" Cupid's Key, 1-1/2" thick.
Belt Course Bracket #1553. Fancy Belt Course, 12" o.c.
Spandrel #4101. 9" Ball & Dowel Spandrel.
Bracket # 1104n9. Quarter Circle Bracket, 9" size, unframed.
Baluster #161-045. Traditional Baluster, 3"x24", 5" on center.
Handrail #201-070. P-3 Rail, with SR3 Subrail #56-020.
Bottom Rail #5605. Sloped-top Bottom Rail, shown with
   center support block.

101.

These large Fretwork Fan Spandrels are quite decorative, but due to their costs, Fretwork (fancy) Spandrels are *more often* used inside the home. For porches, much the same effect can be achieved by placing Brackets beneath a Classic (plain) Spandrel. Still, if the budget allows, it's hard to beat the drama of a Fretwork Spandrel for your porch!

Post #121-065. Traditional 6"x96", with 32" base, 6' on center.
Post Face Bracket #1131. 23" Cupid's Key, 1-1/2" thick.
Belt Course Bracket #1553. Fancy Belt Course, 12" o.c.
Spandrel #4141. 17-3/4" Fan Spandrel.
Baluster #161-045. Traditional Baluster, 3"x24", 6" on center.
Handrail #201-070. P-3 Rail, with SR3 Subrail #56-020.
Bottom Rail #5605. Sloped-top Bottom Rail, shown with
   center support block.

149.

Here we find *two* Spandrels, with Beaded Rail between. The possible combinations are almost endless!

Post #121-065. Traditional 6"x96", with 32" base, 6' on center.
Post Face Bracket #1131. 23" Cupid's Key, 1-1/2" thick.
Belt Course Bracket #1553. Fancy Belt Course, 12" o.c.
Spandrel #4125. 12" Small Ball & Dowel Spandrel.
Spandrel #4133. 8-1/2" Wistaria Spandrel.
Beaded Rail #5610. 1-1/2"x2-1/2".
Sawn Baluster #2327. Urn Baluster, spaced 12" on center.
Handrail #201-135. P-2 Rail, with SR2 Subrail #56-010.
Bottom Rail #5605. Sloped-top Bottom Rail, shown with
  center support block.

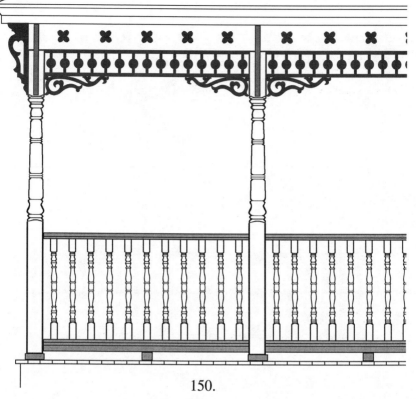

150.

Most of the *Turned* Balusters shown in this section are of the Traditional style. The Heritage style shown here is certainly an alternative, but is only available in a few sizes.

Since the Posts on this porch had *short* tops, we used a long Bracket, turned horizontally, to optimize available space for Gingerbread.

Post #121-062. Traditional 6"x96", with 42" base, 6' on center.
Post Face Bracket #1131. 23" Cupid's Key, 1-1/2" thick, trimmed to fit.
Applique #2422. Dogwood Flower Applique, 12" on center.
Spandrel #4119. 8" Ball & Dowel Spandrel.
Bracket # 1103. 21" Scroll, unframed, horizontal position.
Baluster #161-060. Heritage Baluster, 2"x32", 6" on center.
Handrail #201-135. P-2 Rail, with SR2 Subrail #56-010.
Bottom Rail #5605. Sloped-top Bottom Rail, shown with center support block.

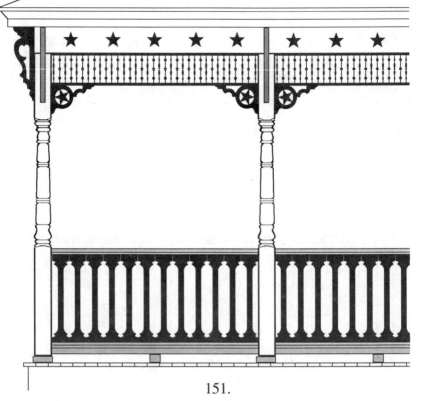

151.

Notice the use of Star Applique, in place of Belt Course Brackets. These can be painted a contrasting color, or left the same color as the Beam to which they are mounted.

The Texas Special Brackets were mounted horizontally. If you prefer, we can adjust their center star (which is sawn from the same piece of wood), so it will point "up" when the Bracket it installed horizontally.

Post #121-065. Traditional 6"x96", with 32" base, 6' on center.
Post Face Bracket #1131. 23" Cupid's Key, 1-1/2" thick.
Applique #2409n4. Star Applique, 4-3/4" size.
Spandrel #4122. 10" Ball & Spindle Spandrel.
Bracket #1150n14. Texas Special, 14" size, unframed.
Baluster #2306. SB#6 Baluster, spaced together.
Handrail #201-135. P-2 Rail, with SR2 Subrail #56-010.
Bottom Rail #5605. Sloped-top Bottom Rail, shown with
  center support block.

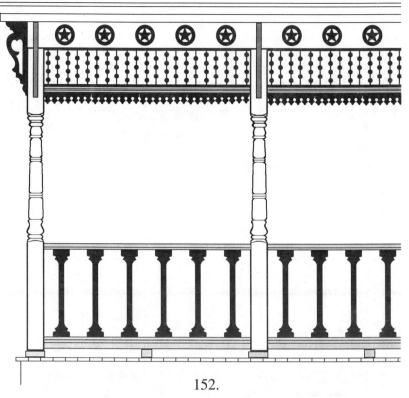

152.

The SB#6 Balusters shown here can be trimmed slightly for height... however, we can easily produce custom lengths (less height through the middle) to exactly fit your needs.

We installed our Running Trim below a Beaded Rail. And although it doesn't really show here, the Running Trim was ordered with a moulded Top Rail. The use of these two Rails gives much more definition to this porch.

Post #121-065. Traditional 6"x96", with 32" base, 6' on center.
Post Face Bracket #1131. 23" Cupid's Key, 1-1/2" thick.
Applique #2401n7. Circle Star, 7" size.
Spandrel #4124. 12" Large Ball & Dowel Spandrel.
Beaded Rail #5610. 1-1/2"x2-1/2".
Running Trim #2206n3. Fleur Running Trim, 3-3/8" size.
Baluster #2306. SB#6 Baluster, 11" on center, trimmed.
Handrail #201-135. P-2 Rail, with SR2 Subrail #56-010.
Bottom Rail #5605. Sloped-top Bottom Rail.

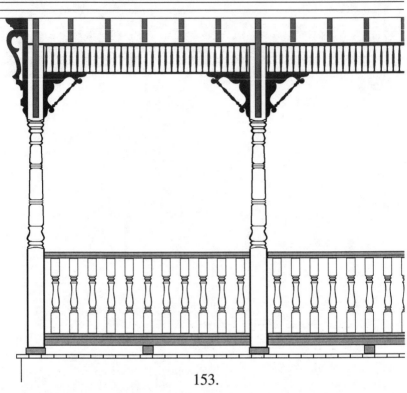

153.

The repetition of turned Spindles and Balusters for Spandrel, Brackets, and Balustrade is harmonious *or* boring, depending upon your point of view!

Post #121-065. Traditional 6"x96", with 32" base, 6' on center.
Post Face Bracket #1132. 31" Cupid's Key, 1-1/2" thick.
Belt Course Bracket #1553. Fancy Belt Course, 12" o.c.
Spandrel #4145. 9-1/2" Spindle Spandrel.
Bracket #1112n13. Flying Spindle Bracket, 13" size, unframed.
Baluster #161-045. Traditional Baluster, 3"x24", 6" on center.
Handrail #201-070. P-3 Rail, with SR3 Subrail #56-020.
Bottom Rail #5605. Sloped-top Bottom Rail.

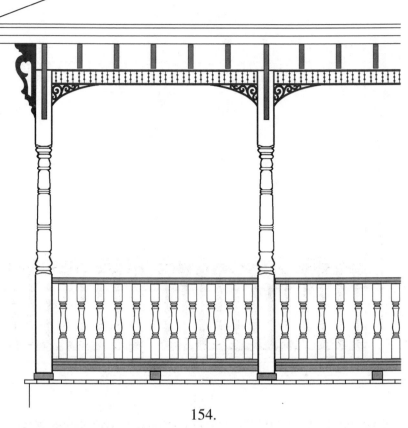

154.

The small Spandrels and Brackets of this porch are very deli-
cate. If this is your intention, it might be well to *also* use 5"
Posts and 2" Balusters.

Post #121-065. Traditional 6"x96", with 32" base, 6' on center.
Post Face Bracket #1131. 23" Cupid's Key, 1-1/2" thick.
Belt Course Bracket #1553. Fancy Belt Course, 12" o.c.
Spandrel #4131. 5" Ball & Dowel Spandrel.
Bracket #1234. Arch Bracket, unframed.
Baluster #161-045. Traditional Baluster, 3"x24", 6" o.c.
Handrail #201-070. P-3 Rail, with SR3 Subrail #56-020.
Bottom Rail #5605. Sloped-top Bottom Rail, shown with
  center support block.

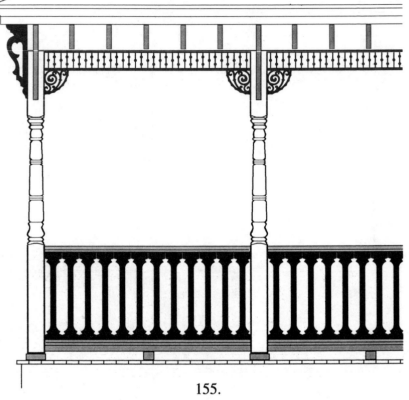

155.

You could "dress up" the Spandrel/Bracket area of this porch by adding a Beaded Rail between them. A somewhat *taller* Bracket might also be considered.

Post #121-065. Traditional 6"x96", with 32" base, 6' on center.
Post Face Bracket #1131. 23" Cupid's Key, 1-1/2" thick.
Belt Course Bracket #1553. Fancy Belt Course, 12" o.c.
Spandrel #4103. 6" Ball & Dowel Spandrel.
Bracket #1241. F.B.#7 Bracket, unframed.
Baluster #2306. SB#6 Baluster, spaced together.
Handrail #201-135. P-2 Rail, with SR2 Subrail #56-010.
Bottom Rail #5605. Sloped-top Bottom Rail, shown with center support block.

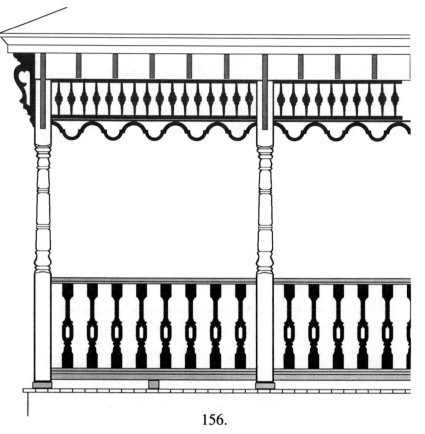

156.

Vine Running Trim, used below the Spandrels, provides a very
different look for this porch. This same Vine can also be used
on the front edge of your house's eaves!

Post #121-065. Traditional 6"x96", with 32" base, 6' on center.
Post Face Bracket #1131. 23" Cupid's Key, 1-1/2" thick.
Belt Course Bracket #1553. Fancy Belt Course, 12" o.c.
Spandrel #4150. 11-3/4" Plain Spool Spandrel.
Running Trim #2208n58. Vine Running Trim.
Baluster #2305. SB#5 Baluster, 8" on center.
Handrail #201-135. P-2 Rail, with SR2 Subrail #56-010.
Bottom Rail #5605. Sloped-top Bottom Rail, shown with
  center support block.

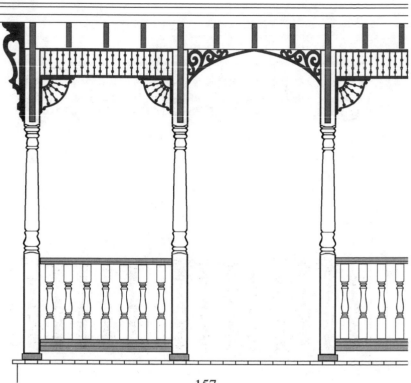

157.

If there's not enough headroom to comfortably pass under your chosen Gingerbread trim, you can do something like this at the entrance(s) to the porch...

In fact, this particular porch *did* have sufficient headroom, but we liked this entryway effect so much, we used it anyway!

Post #121-075. Classic 5"x96", with 32" base, 4' on center.
Post Face Bracket #1132. 31" Cupid's Key, 1-1/2" thick.
Belt Course Bracket #1553. Fancy Belt Course, 12" o.c.
Spandrel #4101. 9" Ball & Dowel Spandrel.
Bracket #1247. Arch Bracket, unframed.
Bracket #1330. 11" - 12 Ball Fan Bracket.
Baluster #161-045. Traditional Baluster, 3"x24", 6" on center.
Handrail #201-070. P-3 Rail, with SR3 Subrail #56-020.
Bottom Rail #5605. Sloped-top Bottom Rail, shown with center support block.

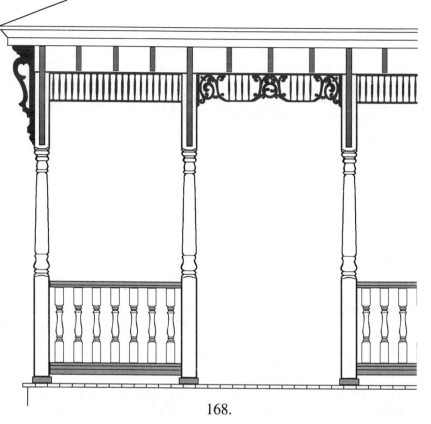

168.

Another way to highlight your porch's entryway is use a single Fretwork Spandrel at the steps, with Classic Spandrels everywhere else.

Post #121-075. Classic 5"x96", with 32" base, 4' on center.
Post Face Bracket #1132. 31" Cupid's Key, 1-1/2" thick.
Belt Course Bracket #1553. Fancy Belt Course, 12" o.c.
Spandrel #4107. Anna Marie Spandrel.
Spandrel #4145. 9-1/2" Spindle Spandrel.
Baluster #161-045. Traditional Baluster, 3"x24", 6" on center.
Handrail #201-070. P-3 Rail, with SR3 Subrail #56-020.
Bottom Rail #5605. Sloped-top Bottom Rail, shown with
  center support block.

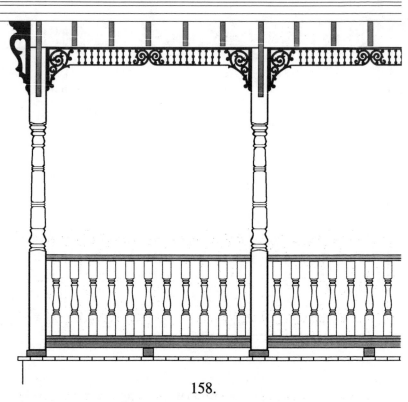

158.

The Fretwork Spandrels used on these two examples are definitely the deluxe approach, but aren't they nice!

Post #121-065. Traditional 6"x96", with 32" base, 6' on center.
Post Face Bracket #1131. 23" Cupid's Key, 1-1/2" thick.
Belt Course Bracket #1553. Fancy Belt Course, 12" o.c.
Spandrel #4105. Eloise Spandrel.
Baluster #161-045. Traditional Baluster, 3"x24", 6" on center.
Handrail #201-070. P-3 Rail, with SR3 Subrail #56-020.
Bottom Rail #5605. Sloped-top Bottom Rail, shown with center support block.

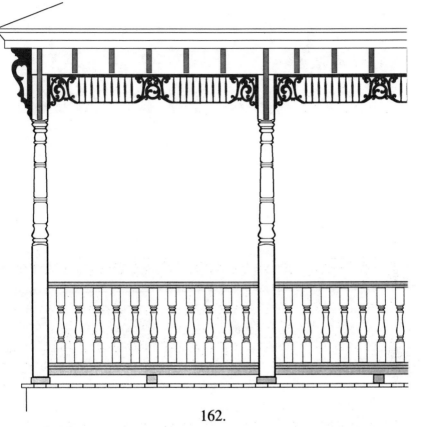

162.

These Anna Marie Spandrels pack a big punch visually, while only being 11" tall overall. They are a good choice for this porch, as the existing Posts only have 14" of square top.

Post #121-062. Traditional 6"x96", with 42" base, 6' on center.
Post Face Bracket #1131. 23" Cupid's Key, 1-1/2" thick, trimmed to fit.
Belt Course Bracket #1553. Fancy Belt Course, 12" o.c.
Spandrel #4107. Anna Marie Spandrel.
Baluster #161-045. Traditional Baluster, 3"x24", 6" on center.
Handrail #201-070. P-3 Rail, with SR3 Subrail #56-020.
Bottom Rail #5605. Sloped-top Bottom Rail, shown with center support block.

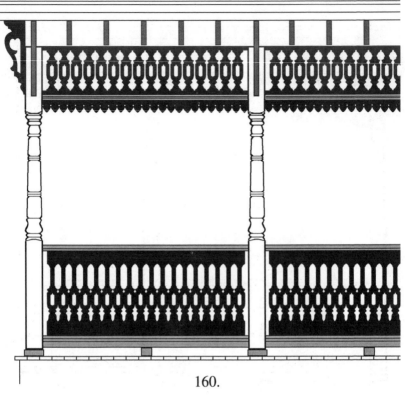

160.

We liked the pattern of the SB#5 Sawn Balusters so much, we commissioned the woodworkers of Vintage Wood Works to create a *Spandrel* from this Baluster design. It's 15" high, including top and bottom rails. This sort of modification to existing items is very cost effective. We've positioned Beaded Rail and Running Trim below the Spandrel.

Post #121-065. Traditional 6"x96", with 32" base, 6' on center.
Post Face Bracket #1131. 23" Cupid's Key, 1-1/2" thick.
Belt Course Bracket #1553. Fancy Belt Course, 12" o.c.
Spandrel. Modified SB#5 (#2305) Sawn Balusters.
Running Trim #2217n3. Picket Running Trim, 3-3/8" size.
Beaded Rail #5610. 1-1/2"x2-1/2".
Baluster #2305. SB#5 Baluster, spaced together.
Handrail #201-135. P-2 Rail, with SR2 Subrail #56-010.
Bottom Rail #5605. Sloped-top Bottom Rail.

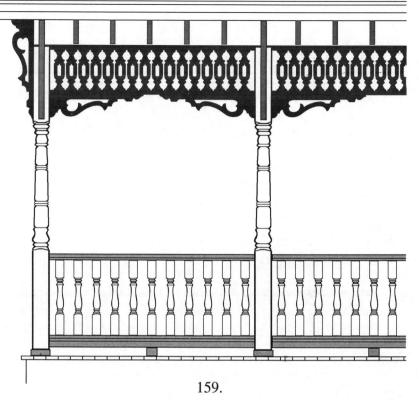

159.

And again we use our newly modified Spandrel, but this time with horizontal Brackets below. We've also changed the balustrade for contrast.

Post #121-065. Traditional 6"x96", with 32" base, 6' on center.
Post Face Bracket #1132. 31" Cupid's Key, 1-1/2" thick.
Belt Course Bracket #1553. Fancy Belt Course, 12" o.c.
Spandrel. Modified SB#5 (#2305) Sawn Balusters.
Bracket #1132. 31" Cupid's Key, 1-1/2" thick, horizontal.
Baluster #161-045. Traditional Baluster, 3"x24", 6" on center.
Handrail #201-070. P-3 Rail, with SR3 Subrail #56-020.
Bottom Rail #5605. Sloped-top Bottom Rail, shown with
  center support block.

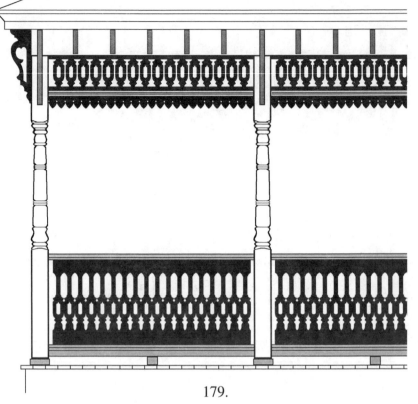

179.

Here we've again modified the SB#5 Baluster for use as a Spandrel, but this time to an even *shorter* version (11" high, including top and bottom rails).

Post #121-065. Traditional 6"x96", with 32" base, 6' on center.
Post Face Bracket #1131. 23" Cupid's Key, 1-1/2" thick.
Belt Course Bracket #1553. Fancy Belt Course, 12" o.c.
Spandrel. Modified SB#5 (#2305) Sawn Balusters.
Running Trim #2217n3. Picket Running Trim, 3-3/8" size.
Beaded Rail #5610. 1-1/2"x2-1/2".
Baluster #2305. SB#5 Baluster, spaced together.
Handrail #201-135. P-2 Rail, with SR2 Subrail #56-010.
Bottom Rail #5605. Sloped-top Bottom Rail, shown with
   center support block.

137.

And once more we've used a shortened SB#5, but this time as part of the Balustrade. We've added Beaded Rail and a second Spandrel to complete our Balustrade, and then repeated the Ball & Dowel Spandrel at the top of the porch.

Post #121-065. Traditional 6"x96", with 32" base, 6' on center.
Post Face Bracket #1132. 31" Cupid's Key, 1-1/2" thick.
Belt Course Bracket #1553. Fancy Belt Course, 12" o.c.
Spandrel #4119. 8" Ball & Dowel Spandrel, used above
    Brackets *and* above Balusters.
Beaded Rail #5610. 1-1/2"x2-1/2".
Bracket #1171. SR#3 Bracket.
Extender #5203. 1-1/2"x2".
Drop #5201n5. 2"x2" Drop, 5-3/4" long.
Baluster #2305. SB#5 Baluster, modified, spaced together.
Handrail #201-135. P-2 Rail, with SR2 Subrail #56-010.
Bottom Rail #5605. Sloped-top Bottom Rail.

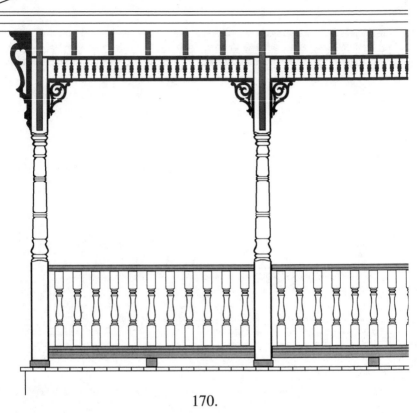

170.

These two pages illustrate subtle differences achieved by changing Bracket and Spandrel sizes, and by turning the Brackets vertically or horizontally.

Post #121-065. Traditional 6"x96", with 32" base, 6' on center.
Post Face Bracket #1132. 31" Cupid's Key, 1-1/2" thick.
Belt Course Bracket #1553. Fancy Belt Course, 12" o.c.
Spandrel #4127. 7" Spool Spandrel.
Bracket #1243n10. F.B.#8, 10" size, framed.
Baluster #161-045. Traditional Baluster, 3"x24", 6" on center.
Handrail #201-070. P-3 Rail, with SR3 Subrail #56-020.
Bottom Rail #5605. Sloped-top Bottom Rail, shown with center support block.

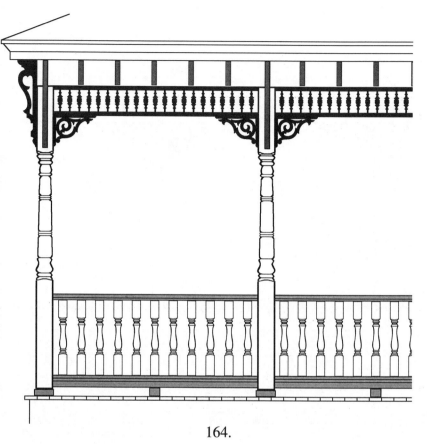

164.

Here the Brackets and Spandrels are one size larger...

Post #121-065. Traditional 6"x96", with 32" base, 6' on center.
Post Face Bracket #1132. 31" Cupid's Key, 1-1/2" thick.
Belt Course Bracket #1553. Fancy Belt Course, 12" o.c.
Spandrel #4128. 10" Spool Spandrel.
Bracket #1243n12. F.B.#8, 12" size, horizontal position, framed.
Baluster #161-045. Traditional Baluster, 3"x24", 6" on center.
Handrail #201-070. P-3 Rail, with SR3 Subrail #56-020.
Bottom Rail #5605. Sloped-top Bottom Rail, shown with center support block.

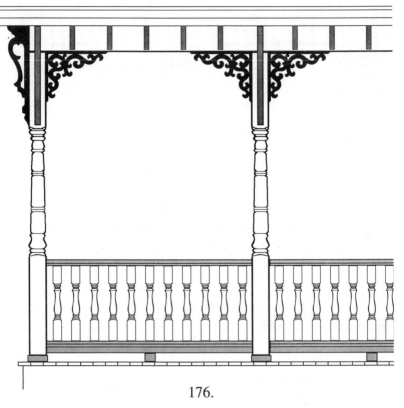

176.

Generally, we favor the use of Spandrels (if the budget permits) but larger Brackets, as shown on these two pages, can be very effective used alone.

Post #121-065. Traditional 6"x96", with 32" base, 6' on center.
Post Face Bracket #1132. 31" Cupid's Key, 1-1/2" thick.
Belt Course Bracket #1553. Fancy Belt Course, 12" o.c.
Bracket #1238. Stockbridge Bracket, framed.
Baluster #161-045. Traditional Baluster, 3"x24", 6" on center.
Handrail #201-070. P3 Rail, with SR3 Subrail #56-020.
Bottom Rail #5605. Sloped-top Bottom Rail, shown with
  center support block.

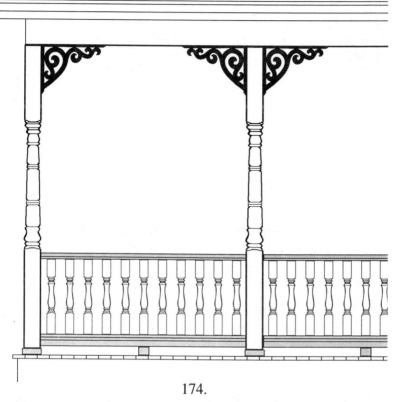

174.

However, we've *omitted* Post Face and Belt Course Brackets from this example... and in so doing, we've lost the "third dimension" that would make this porch so pleasing in real life!

Post #121-065. Traditional 6"x96", with 32" base, 6' on center.
Bracket #1239. Archredeux Bracket, framed.
Baluster #161-045. Traditional Baluster, 3"x24", 6" on center.
Handrail #201-070. P-3 Rail, with SR3 Subrail #56-020.
Bottom Rail #5605. Sloped-top Bottom Rail, shown with center support block.

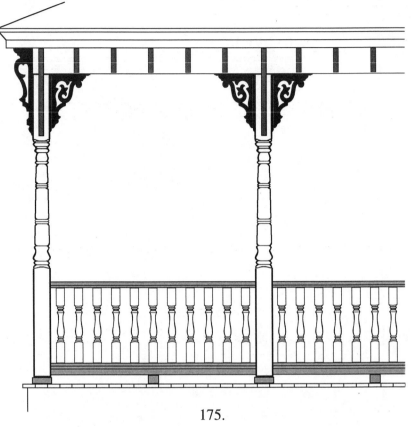

175.

Again, we're showing Brackets without Spandrels, but we've restored our "third dimension" with Post Face and Belt Course Brackets.

Post #121-060. Traditional 6"x96", with 36" base, 6' on center.
Post Face Bracket #1132. 27" Cupid's Key, 1-1/2" thick.
Belt Course Bracket #1553. Fancy Belt Course, 12" o.c.
Bracket #1116. Fleur Bracket, framed.
Baluster #161-045. Traditional Baluster, 3"x24", 6" on center.
Handrail #201-070. P-3 Rail, with SR3 Subrail #56-020.
Bottom Rail #5605. Sloped-top Bottom Rail, shown with
  center support block.

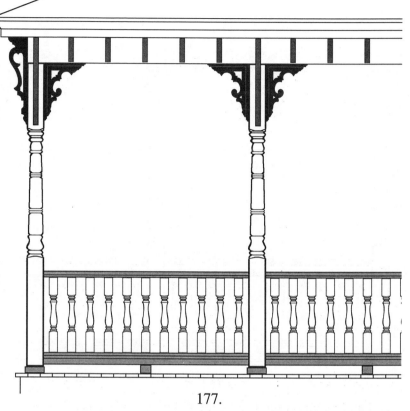

177.

These Triangle E Brackets also work very well turned horizontally, but that's true of most Brackets!

Post #121-060. Traditional 6"x96", with 36" base, 6' on center.
Post Face Bracket #1132. 27" Cupid's Key, 1-1/2" thick.
Belt Course Bracket #1553. Fancy Belt Course, 12" o.c.
Bracket #1106. Triangle E Bracket, framed.
Baluster #161-045. Traditional Baluster, 3"x24", 6" on center.
Handrail #201-070. P-3 Rail, with SR3 Subrail #56-020.
Bottom Rail #5605. Sloped-top Bottom Rail, shown with center support block.

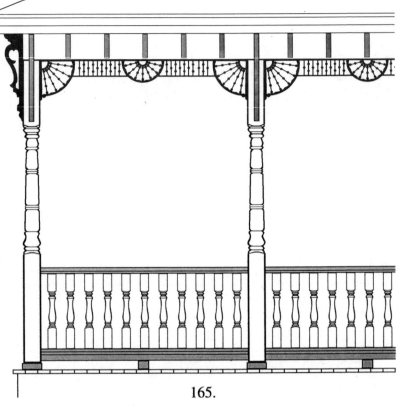

165.

The Fan Spandrel used here is relatively expensive per foot, as it's built to exact lengths. All components are skillfully joined at Vintage Wood Works' shop into complete units, exactly fitting the spaces between each pair of Porch Posts.

Post #121-060. Traditional 6"x96", with 36" base, 6' on center.
Post Face Bracket #1132. 27" Cupid's Key, 1-1/2" thick.
Belt Course Bracket #1553. Fancy Belt Course, 12" o.c.
Spandrel #4140. 13-3/4" Fan Spandrel.
Baluster #161-045. Traditional Baluster, 3"x24", 6" on center.
Handrail #201-070. P-3 Rail, with SR3 Subrail #56-020.
Bottom Rail #5605. Sloped-top Bottom Rail, shown with
  center support block.

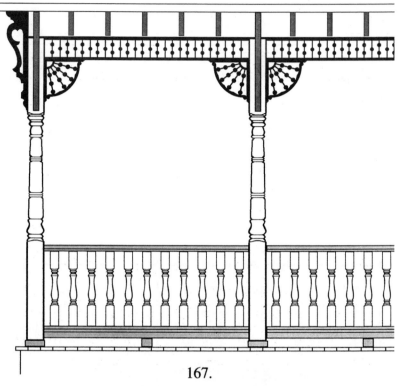

167.

In contrast, this porch uses Classic Spandrels that are quite a bit *less* per foot. By installing Fan Brackets below, we duplicate most of the charm of porch #165, while saving budget for other items.

Post #121-065. Traditional 6"x96", with 32" base, 6' on center.
Post Face Bracket #1132. 31" Cupid's Key, 1-1/2" thick.
Belt Course Bracket #1553. Fancy Belt Course, 12" o.c.
Spandrel #4120. 7" Ball & Dowel Spandrel.
Bracket #1384. 13-3/4" - 12 Ball Fan Bracket.
Baluster #161-045. Traditional Baluster, 3"x24", 6" on center.
Handrail #201-070. P-3 Rail, with SR3 Subrail #56-020.
Bottom Rail #5605. Sloped-top Bottom Rail, shown with center support block.

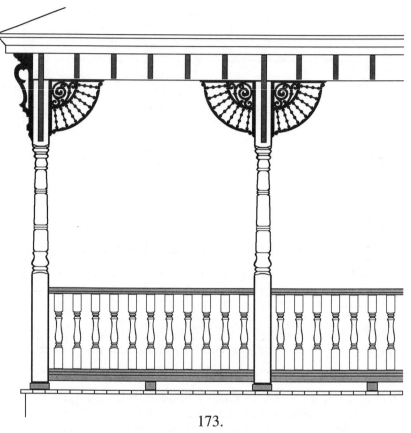

173.

These larger Fan Brackets look fine without Spandrels.

Post #121-060. Traditional 6"x96", with 36" base, 6' on center.
Post Face Bracket #1132. 27" Cupid's Key, 1-1/2" thick.
Belt Course Bracket #1553. Fancy Belt Course, 12" o.c.
Bracket #1329. 28 Ball Fan Bracket.
Baluster #161-045. Traditional Baluster, 3"x24", 6" on center.
Handrail #201-070. P-3 Rail, with SR3 Subrail #56-020.
Bottom Rail #5605. Sloped-top Bottom Rail, shown with center support block.

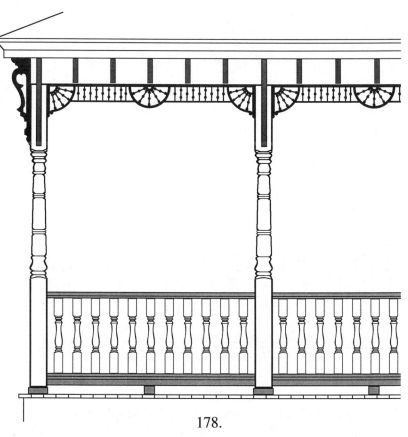

178.

And here's another size of Fan Spandrel for your consideration...

Post #121-060. Traditional 6"x96", with 36" base, 6' on center.
Post Face Bracket #1132. 27" Cupid's Key, 1-1/2" thick.
Belt Course Bracket #1553. Fancy Belt Course, 12" o.c.
Spandrel #4139. 11" Fan Spandrel.
Baluster #161-045. Traditional Baluster, 3"x24", 6" on center.
Handrail #201-070. P-3 Rail, with SR3 Subrail #56-020.
Bottom Rail #5605. Sloped-top Bottom Rail, shown with
center support block.

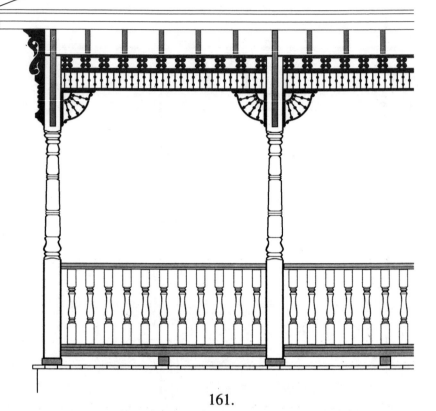

161.

The Dogwood Spandrel added to this example provides interesting contrast to the ball and dowel work of the other Spandrel and of the Fan Brackets. Please also notice the marvelous Post Face Bracket used for this porch.

Post #121-065. Traditional 6"x96", with 32" base, 6' on center.
Post Face Bracket #1125. Ruffled Swan, 1-1/2" thick.
Belt Course Bracket #1553. Fancy Belt Course, 12" o.c.
Spandrel #4136. Dogwood Spandrel.
Spandrel #4103. 6" Ball & Dowel Spandrel.
Bracket #1330. 11" - 12 Ball Fan Bracket.
Baluster #161-045. Traditional Baluster, 3"x24", 6" on center.
Handrail #201-070. P-3 Rail, with SR3 Subrail #56-020.
Bottom Rail #5605. Sloped-top Bottom Rail, shown with
  center support block.

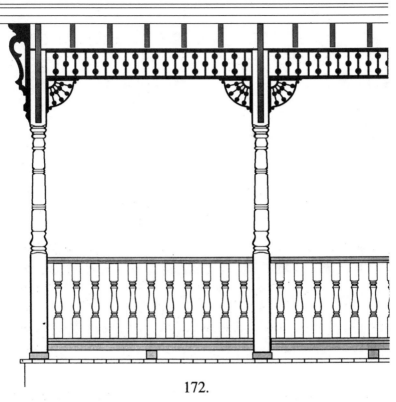

172.

The balls and dowels of this example are a bit heavier than the past several examples.

Post #121-065. Traditional 6"x96", with 32" base, 6' on center.
Post Face Bracket #1132. 31" Cupid's Key, 1-1/2" thick.
Belt Course Bracket #1553. Fancy Belt Course, 12" o.c.
Spandrel #4117. 8-3/4" Ball & Dowel Spandrel.
Bracket #1385. 11" - 8 Ball Fan Bracket.
Baluster #161-045. Traditional Baluster, 3"x24", 6" on center.
Handrail #201- 070. P-3 Rail, with SR3 Subrail #56-020.
Bottom Rail #5605. Sloped-top Bottom Rail, shown with
  center support block.

169.

The Virginia Creeper Bracket used here provides a very distinctive look... almost organic!

Post #121-060. Traditional 6"x96", with 36" base, 6' on center.
Post Face Bracket #1132. 27" Cupid's Key, 1-1/2" thick.
Belt Course Bracket #1553. Fancy Belt Course, 12" o.c.
Bracket #1128n17. Virginia Creeper, 17" size, unframed.
Baluster #161-045. Traditional Baluster, 3"x24", 6" on center.
Handrail #201-070. P-3 Rail, with SR3 Subrail #56-020.
Bottom Rail #5605. Sloped-top Bottom Rail, shown with center support block.

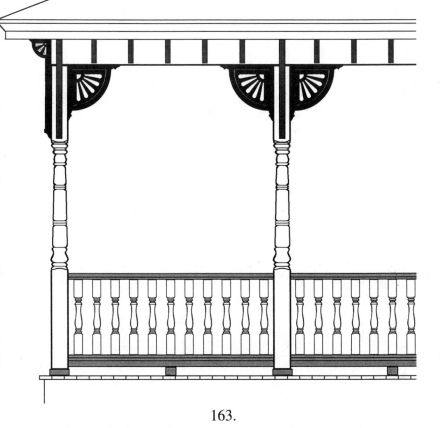

163.

The citrus motif of these Brackets is repeated in the design at the top of the Post Face Bracket.

Post #121-065. Traditional 6"x96", with 32" base, 6' on center.
Post Face Bracket #3120. 31" Citrus Top, 3" thick.
Belt Course Bracket #1553. Fancy Belt Course, 12" o.c.
Bracket #1122n17. Citrus Bracket, 17" size.
Baluster #161-045. Traditional Baluster, 3"x24", 6" on center.
Handrail #201-070. P-3 Rail, with SR3 Subrail #56-020.
Bottom Rail #5605. Sloped-top Bottom Rail, shown with
  center support block.

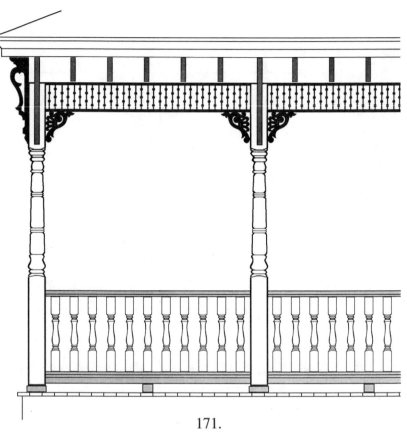

171.

Both these porches are attractive and well balanced. This one achieves its good looks with straight forward Brackets and Spandrels...

Post #121-060. Traditional 6"x96", with 36" base, 6' on center.
Post Face Bracket #1132. 27" Cupid's Key, 1-1/2" thick.
Belt Course Bracket #1553. Fancy Belt Course, 12" o.c.
Spandrel #4101. 9" Ball & Dowel Spandrel.
Bracket #1124n9. Cockscomb Bracket, 9" size, unframed.
Baluster #161-045. Traditional Baluster, 3"x24", 6" on center.
Handrail #201-070. P-3 Rail, with SR3 Subrail #56-020.
Bottom Rail #5605. Sloped-top Bottom Rail, shown with center support block.

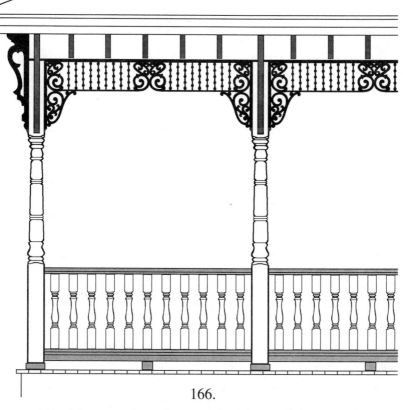

166.

... while this example makes wonderful use of the very decorative Mary Elizabeth Fretwork Spandrel.

Post #121-065. Traditional 6"x96", with 32" base, 6' on center.
Post Face Bracket #1132. 31" Cupid's Key, 1-1/2" thick.
Belt Course Bracket #1553. Fancy Belt Course, 12" o.c.
Spandrel #4110. Mary Elizabeth Spandrel.
Baluster #161-045. Traditional Baluster, 3"x24", 6" on center.
Handrail #201-070. P-3 Rail, with SR3 Subrail #56-020.
Bottom Rail #5605. Sloped-top Bottom Rail, shown with center support block.

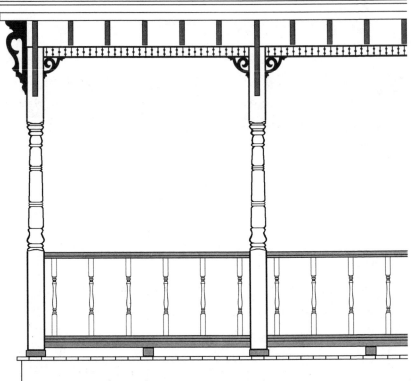

135.

This porch has two problems. First, the Balusters are too far apart, particularly for the narrower 2" size Balusters selected. Second, the Spandrels, and Brackets beneath them, are too small. Nevertheless, this porch is far better than the next one...

Post #121-065. Traditional 6"x96", with 32" base, 6' on center.
Post Face Bracket #1131. 23" Cupid's Key, 1-1/2" thick.
Belt Course Bracket #1553. Fancy Belt Course, 12" o.c.
Spandrel #4144. 3-1/2" Ball & Dowel Spandrel.
Bracket #1104n7. Quarter Circle, 7" size, unframed.
Baluster #161-020. Traditional Baluster, 2"x24", 12" o.c.
Handrail #201-135. P-2 Rail, with SR2 Subrail #56-010.
Bottom Rail #5605. Sloped-top Bottom Rail, shown with
   center support block.

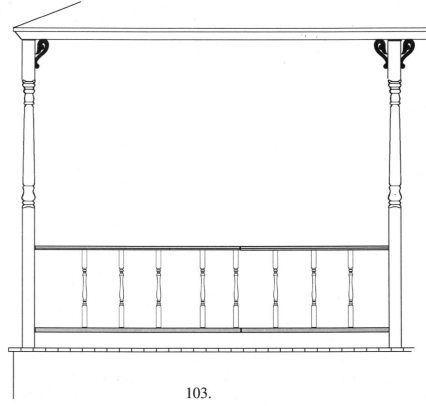

103.

Our final example is "The No-No Porch". We're pleased *you* know better! This porch has the following problems:

- Skimpy fascia (eave) and no Beam.
- Post Tops cut short, rather than removing excess Post length from the base area (or ordering more appropriate Posts to begin with).
- Brackets too small, even for the limited Post top area.
- 4" size of Posts too small for the wide spacing.
- Posts installed without Base Blocks or Base Mounting Plates. Water damage to follow...
- No Subrail, giving the Handrail a weak appearance.
- Use of *interior* style bottom railing, rather than our correct Sloped-Top Bottom Rail. Water damage to follow...
- Balusters too far apart for this 2" size.
- Balusters spaced unevenly, and too far from the Posts.
- Short pieces of Handrail and Bottom Rail, with weak joints.
- No Support Block under Bottom Rail.

Chapter Three

Designing Your Porch

Congratulations!   You now know more about the porch and its components than many professionals. It's understandable if your head is reeling a bit right about now.   **Take heart... the fun is about to begin!**

It was necessary for us to present the previous sections in Chapter II so that you would have a firm foundation upon which to make decisions concerning the design of your *own* Magnificent Porch! With this knowledge you are now ready to thoughtfully and skillfully design a beautifully proportioned, enjoyable, and permanent addition to your home.

Don't hesitate to refer to these previous sections as you formulate your own porch design.   We've purposely arranged this book in a logical manner to serve as a permanent reference work for you. Please also note the very complete Index at the end of this book.

And, as always, we're as close as your phone for free consultation... (903) 356-2158.

Initial Considerations

Here are some points to consider in determining the size and configuration of your porch:

1. How is your porch to be used?
Will it primarily serve as a covered passage? Do you envision close family gatherings occasionally? Will the porch be an extension of your home's living area when you are entertaining larger numbers of guests?

2. What, if any, furnishings will be placed on the porch?
Porch swings, rocking chairs, a breakfast table, firewood, or potted plants are just a few of many fixtures you may wish to use; all of which require space.

3. What size and configuration should your porch be to complement the building to which it will be attached?
Understandably, the design of your porch must accommodate your foreseen needs. But also your porch must "fit" with its surroundings. It should aesthetically complement and enhance the home in both proportion and size.

Consider the size and style of the home or building to which the porch will be attached. Then drive by examples of porches from the turn of the century or older. Analyze why some porches look very much a part of the overall structure, and why some look rather "tacked-on"!

4. Is this to be a remodeling of an existing porch?
If so, please see The Porch Remodeling Section of **Chapter I.**

5. What style and amount of Gingerbread do you want?
The Posts (both Porch and Newel), the Balustrade, the Post Top Items, and the Porch Eave Decorations... together these four main categories of porch decoration will determine the final style, balance, and visual effectiveness of your porch... even more than the basic porch structure. It is important that these four categories of decoration work together. The finished porch should make one complete "statement".

A MODERATE APPROACH

Gingerbread can cover quite a range, from simple and sparse to intricate and plentiful. A moderate approach, somewhere between the two ends of this scale, is typically the most appropriate. Consider for a moment the overall style of the home this porch will belong to. If a three story Queen Anne Victorian, with high roof lines, soaring gables, and perhaps even a circular tower is involved, your Gingerbread will appear inadequate unless it is both intricate in detail and quite abundant! Conversely, a very modest home, with simple lines and shallow roof, may seem overdone if its porch appears to have been transplanted from one of the High Victorians described above.

However, most homes fall *between* these two extremes. If your home is in this middle area, your decorating is actually easier, because you can properly decorate your porch within a broad range, from fairly minimal to rather involved. Which degree (and style) of decoration you choose under such circumstances depends upon the direction in which you may wish to change your home's overall style.

DON'T BE TOO CONSERVATIVE

Nevertheless, it has been our observation over the years that, when choosing Gingerbread for one's home, the tendency is to be *too* conservative! More often than not, one's concern for *overdoing it* limits the truly effective use of decorative trim items. Obviously, it *is* possible to overdo it, but all too often we see people reordering *more* decoration because they were not quite satisfied with the initial results. Remember, all items will seem much smaller when viewed from the distance of the street. And, if properly selected and installed, the various Gingerbread items will blend together into one *whole.*

We will later cover specific ways you can test for these matters before you order, but the point we are trying to stress here is that often just a little more (or larger) trim could make a big difference in the overall impact. *Don't be afraid to trust your own decorating judgement.* After all, it *is* your home!

BUDGET CONSIDERATIONS

As you will discover, we are very eager to maintain the cost effectiveness of your Gingerbread. We will *never* advise additional (or more expensive) items unless we sincerely believe they will add more to the value of your home than what they cost. We firmly believe the purchase of any decorative porch trim can and should be viewed as an investment. (Although admittedly, one of the few investments that can also be enjoyed for its non-monetary aspects.)

Of course, budget constraints are often a very real factor. We feel strongly, however, that it is better to do part of the project well, and come back later when the budget allows, rather than to spread the pocketbook too thin, and have the entire project displease you! For example, we would favor a structurally sound porch with no decoration at first, rather than a poorly constructed porch that may require a redo at a later date.

WAYS TO STRETCH YOUR DOLLARS
There are many ways to make the initial budget go farther:

A. Build the porch the *depth* you want, but limit its *length*, adding more later.

B. Purchase the correctly sized Posts, and in adequate quantity, but wait until later to add the Gingerbread. It's very important, of course, to determine initially that your Posts will accommodate this later Gingerbread. Please see the section titled THE POSTS, Chapter II for more details.

C. Install Balustrades now if required for safety considerations, but wait to add the remaining decoration.

D. If you want Spandrels with Brackets beneath, but the budget is tight, put up only the Brackets at first (using easily removable screws). If you allow room now for the spandrels to be added, it will be a simple matter to later remove the Brackets, install the Spandrels, and then replace the Brackets below the Spandrels!

E. As mentioned previously, we strongly recommend the use of Post Face Brackets and Porch Eave Brackets (Belt Course Brackets) to provide that all important *third* dimension to your porch... but these may be added at a later date.

In other words, if you begin with a plan, and know from the start that your design will properly accommodate the various elements you ultimately want, it is always possible to work in stages.   In fact, it gives you something to look forward to... and this approach can easily answer the question of what to give each other for Christmas, Birthdays, Anniversaries, and surprises!

The Plan

A good way to start planning your new porch is with a package of graph paper.   Decide how many inches each square on the paper will represent (the scale of the drawing), and note this at the top of your page.   You will also need a sharp pencil, a straight-edged instrument (such as a ruler), and a metal measuring tape.

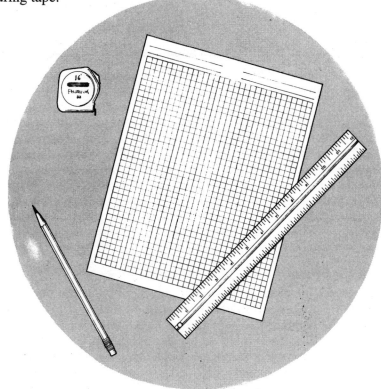

49. Let's draw a "plan" of your porch!

Armed with the aforementioned tools, we are going to draw a floor plan of your porch... not unlike one that might be prepared by an architect or building designer. A "plan" is basically a layout, drawn as if viewing your porch from directly above. The drawings at the start of Chapter II are examples of "plans".

EXISTING CONDITIONS

With your metal tape, measure the length of the wall (or walls) of the building to which your porch will be attached. (Of course, if you are planning a porch for a building not yet constructed, you will need to use the proposed plan for this building to determine the length of wall to which your porch will be attached.) Draw a line(s) to represent this wall(s), being careful to apply the scale you have decided upon. Locate all doors and windows and transfer them to your drawing. What we are trying to achieve is a graphical representation of existing conditions.

THE LENGTH

Next we must decide upon a *tentative* length for your porch, based upon existing conditions.

The overall balance of porch and main structure is the most important factor. It is often more visually pleasing for a porch to end a foot or two short of the corner of the building to which it is attached. We are only determining a *tentative* length at this point, for we may soon find that slightly more or less length will work better when the spacing of steps, posts, etc. are considered. For now, it is the *approximate* length of your porch we are needing. Once you determine this length, so indicate with marks on your drawing.

THE DEPTH

The depth, front to back, of your porch can vary from less than enough for sitting (for decorative purposes only!) to extra deep. For most porches, this depth will be eight to ten feet. This allows plenty of room for swings, chairs and small tables. Decide upon a *tentative* depth, and draw this onto your plan.

THE STEPS

The next most important consideration is the position of the steps, both for the primary entrance to the porch, and for any secondary steps you may desire.

If the porch is to have a low concrete slab foundation, steps, in the traditional sense, may not be required. In that case, the present discussion of step location should be interpreted to mean the location of the walkway, opening in the Balustrade, or opening in the flower beds that would determine the point at which one would step onto the porch.

Generally, the main entrance steps will be directly in front of the main entrance to the building, assuming this is a *front* porch. For side or rear porches, it is often more convenient for the main steps of the porch to be located at a position other than directly in front of the entrance to this side of the building.

Mark *temporarily* on your plan the location of the primary (and any secondary) steps you would like to have. Indicate the width of opening onto the porch that these steps will require. (There is, of course, no absolute rule of thumb for how wide steps should be, but certainly the primary steps should be of sufficient width to allow two people to pass one another.)

THE POSTS
Now we are ready to determine the tentative placement of the Posts (both Porch and Newel). For reasons that will become apparent shortly, this is one of the most important aspects of designing your porch!

*The following discussion does **not** take into account structural considerations. We cannot make these determinations for you, but generally, for standard porch construction, Porch Posts can be spaced up to ten feet apart. It is typically not the strength of the Posts, but of the beam above, that limits such spacing. If you are unsure of the structural aspects involved, please seek the advice of a qualified contractor, architect, or structural engineer.*

Our goal is to have the same distance separating each pair of Porch Posts... but you should be forewarned that exact symmetry is seldom possible! (Note - if your porch will turn a corner, then it is desirable to have the same distance between Porch Posts on *each* side of the porch. Also, the absolute optimum condition is to have the distance between Porch Posts equal the depth of the porch, so that the corner Posts will be this same distance from the wall of the building. Fortunately, this last point is much less important.) There are several considerations to be made in determining the proper placement of Posts:

• We must have a Porch Post at each corner of the porch.

• We must have either a full length Porch Post or a Newel Post on either side of any steps or entryway.

• We want to avoid having a Porch Post in front of any door or window, if possible.

• It is more visually pleasing to use Half Posts against walls.

• An intermediate Newel Post *may* be used between each pair of Porch Posts, if desired.

Please notice that the above list includes two *"must haves"* (Posts at each corner and at either side of steps), one *"want"* (Posts clear of windows or doors), and two *"options"* (Half Posts, and intermediate Newel Posts.

Let's start by *temporarily* marking your plan with a "P" for the location of each corner Porch Post. If using them, also mark an "H" for the position of Half Posts. If you'll have Newel Posts to provide an opening for steps, then mark those locations with an "N" (otherwise mark a "P" where Porch Posts will be used on either side of each set of steps.) Now, with corners and steps located, let's see if we can determine *intermediate* Porch Post positions that will satisfy our goal of having equal spacing between all Porch Posts, while *also* not having any Porch Posts in front of windows or doors. (It will usually work from an aesthetic standpoint to have between five and ten feet between Porch Posts.)

If you can easily position your intermediate Porch Post to meet all of our parameters, consider yourself lucky and move on to the next section on Elevations!

For the other 99% of all porches, let's see what can be done to optimize your somewhat uneven Porch Post spacing:

- Consider making your steps a different width.

- For secondary steps, consider relocating them.

- If you've used Porch Posts to the side of your steps, consider substituting Newel Posts. You can be somewhat arbitrary in deciding how much distance to have between these Newels and your Porch Posts. Thus, you will have some flexibility in determining the position of the intermediate Porch Posts.

- Consider changing the overall length of your porch.

- If your house is not yet built, consider changing the position of windows and doors.

- If your porch turns a corner, consider using a different total number of intermediate Porch Posts, in the hope that this may help to equalize the space between Posts from one side of the porch to the other.

And after all of these consideration, if you still are unable to achieve exactly equal spacing between your Porch Posts, take heart. As long as you are reasonably close, you are probably the only one that will ever know. *We won't tell if you don't!*

The Elevations

An *elevation* is another type of drawing you will find very useful. It is drawn as though you were viewing *one* face of the porch from directly in front of you. Thus, everything will be two dimensional. For example, if you are drawing the Beam above the Posts, you will show only the *face* of the Beam. Likewise, only the *face* of the Posts will show. (If you were drawing to show the *third* dimension, then you would be making a perspective drawing, but perspectives are better left to artists and draftspersons. Of course, if you are an artist or draftsperson, have at it... your time will be well spent!

You'll want to draw a front and both side elevations. Then you'll be able to see what your porch will look like viewed from the front and from either side. You will be richly rewarded for the time and effort expended on the elevations, as it is always much easier to change your mind on paper!

EXISTING CONDITIONS
Again, we need to establish the existing conditions. With your metal tape, measure the height of the wall (or walls) of the building to which your porch will be attached. (You can "read" your floor plan to determine the length of this existing wall.)

We will begin with the front elevation. Using the same scale you established for your floor plan, draw light lines representing the ground level, and the length and height of the building side to which your porch will be attached. Locate all doors and windows, and transfer them to your elevation, showing how tall they are. (Use the bottom of the door(s) as your baseline, because the floor of the porch will be just slightly below this level.) Use a light touch to your pencil, as we will want to erase portions of these lines as we proceed.

It is important that you take reasonable care in producing this graphical representation of existing conditions onto your elevation. The ultimate success of your porch depends upon the accuracy you are establishing now!

A QUICK SKETCH
Once you are satisfied with your portrayal of existing conditions, we can draw in the porch itself. But at this point it is often helpful to set aside for a moment our actual elevation, and work from a rough sketch. **We need to verify that our intended porch is going to work!** To do this, let's make a quick, rough copy of our elevation. (If a copier is handy, run a quick copy on the machine.)

Sketch onto your copy the length and height of the intended porch, indicating the floor line, steps, roof line, Posts, and the Beam above the Posts. Try to use roughly the scale of your elevation in making this sketch. Then you can verify certain rough measurements, such as the length of your Porch Posts.

We are drawing just enough to represent the porch as it would be *before* adding any decorative trim. Sketch in the roof line in sufficient detail to assure that the wall(s) of the existing building are high enough to accept your porch along its entire length.

You may need to make several adjustments to this quick sketch before all of the porch elements are in harmony. Do not be concerned with neatness at this point; we merely need to get a quick idea of how our porch "fits" its building! **Once you are satisfied with this quick sketch, let's move back to your "official" elevation...**

THE FLOOR

Begin with a line to represent the floor of the porch. Remember, for most porches, the floor is set an inch or two below the bottom of the door(s) of the building to which the porch is attached. This allows proper water drainage. If your porch floor is to be of wood, you may want a second line on your Elevation to indicate the *thickness* of the floor.

THE FOUNDATION

Draw in your representation of the foundation the porch floor rests on. (You may want to refer to the section on *Structural Porch Components*, Chapter II, for a discussion on types of foundations, or you can skip drawing in the foundation until later.)

THE POSTS

Now draw the Posts, both Porch and Newel. Refer to your floor plan for locations. Typically, Porch Posts are set in slightly from the edge of the floor. If the floor is to be of wood, it will normally overhang the structure below it by about 1", and the Porch Posts are then set back from the edge of the floor by this same amount, allowing them to rest firmly on the underlying structure. Using your previously determined scale, draw in the Posts so that you are representing their *thickness*, as well as their height.

THE BEAM

Draw in the Beam above the Porch Posts.

THE EAVE

Referring again to Chapter II if necessary, draw in the over-hanging eave of your porch. Remember, since we are still working on the front elevation (by definition, only two dimensional), all that your drawing will show is the face of the eave. This board is called the fascia. Our interest here is in seeing the balance between the depth of the fascia, the depth of the Beam, and the depth of the porch roof.

THE ROOF LINE

Drawing the roof line is easier than it might seem, since again you are only concerned with the view directly from the front. Most porch roofs will look more traditional if they are "hipped". By that we mean that they do *not* have triangular gables at their ends. Rather, the roof "wraps" around the end of the porch. *The choice of roof style is up to you.*

50. Porch with hipped roof.

A REVIEW OF THE FRONT ELEVATION

Pause for a few moments to study the elevation you have just drawn...

• Review again the checklist earlier in this Chapter concerning placement of Porch Posts. Verify that a pleasing symmetry has been achieved.

• Have you been able to avoid placing Porch Posts in front of windows or doors?

• Does the porch, as you have drawn it on your elevation, match the dimensions and layout of your floor plan?

• Does your porch meet your original goals, as set forth in the *Initial Considerations* section toward the first of this Chapter?

• Are there trees or other obstructions that would prevent the porch being built as you have it drawn?

• Do you need secondary steps to access a side yard?

• In short, are you looking at a drawing of your *Dream Porch*? If not, it is much easier to make your changes now! Often setting your plan and elevation aside for a day or two will give you renewed inspiration. Remember, as we quoted in the opening pages of this book...

> *Take your time.*
> *Enjoy the work as you proceed.*

(You should not expect of yourself that you can, in one burst of energy, create your finished masterpiece.)

> *Life is not merely results, however grand,*
> *But mainly the thoughts, the actions, and*
> *The individual moments leading to a goal.*

(View the planning, the design, and the drawing phases as some of the fun, part of the challenge, and much of the joy that you can derive from this project!)

Your added bonus is the joy, the satisfaction,
And the memory of a job well done.

THE GINGERBREAD

If all appears well with your front elevation, you should now draw in the anticipated decorative components. This will allow you the opportunity to further verify that everything will fit on the actual porch! We do *not* need an artistic rendition at this point, as we are concerned with fit and overall balance, not your drawing skills (or lack thereof!). Therefore, you may represent the decorative components as triangles and rectangles.

You will probably want to refer at this time to the sections in **Chapter II** on *Decorative Porch Components* and *Porch Examples* as a refresher on the possibilities available for your porch. Remember, your elevation is very easy to change. Don't hesitate to experiment with various combinations of trim. For future reference, it is a good idea to indicate on your elevation the stock numbers of the items you are tentatively selecting.

When selecting your Gingerbread, please pay particular attention to the distance from porch floor to bottom of trim items over the steps. (A standard door opening is 6' 8" tall.) Unless your family includes a very tall person, it is generally permissible to fudge a little, but 6' 6" should be about the shortest clearance.

The Folks at Vintage Wood Works consider themselves experts on the selection of decorative items for porches. Please do not hesitate to give us a call if we can be of any assistance...

(903) 356-2158.

SIDE ELEVATIONS

You should also take the time to draw side elevations, showing a view of your porch as seen from either end. Follow the same steps you have just used for the front elevation.

Typically, your decorative items will continue to the wall of the building to which the porch is attached. Thus, a Bracket (if Brackets are used on the front of the porch) will also be used against this wall. You will recall that this is the situation for which we earlier recommended the use of a Half Porch Post to provide a more finished look where Porch and building connect.

Chapter Four

Ordering Materials

Ordering the materials for your porch is our next step...

While it is best to procure the purely **structural** components locally, Vintage Wood Works does stock one of the largest selections of Porch Posts available anywhere. *Our prices for Posts are such that it is typically less expensive (shipping included) to order directly from us.*

NEIGHBORLY SERVICE

Vintage Wood Works carries a very extensive inventory of just about all of the decorative items that any porch could need. Even custom length items (made to your specific requirements) are promptly available for shipping. Our goal has always been to provide "neighborly" service, as if we were located just across the back fence! We like to think that dealing with Vintage Wood Works should actually be easier than getting these items locally, assuming they can be found locally...

After all, we have more selection, inventory, experience, production capacity, and old-fashioned service than anyone else.

"Bringing Back Yesterday in Quality & Service" is more than just our slogan.   Even if you *were* lucky enough to have a retired master woodworker close by, we don't think he could do the job as well as we, since we're specialists (and the recognized leaders) in this field!

As we state in our Catalogue:

Each day we prove again that quality small-town custom woodworking and national shipping schedules can be combined... and we're careful to throw in plenty of old-fashioned value and genuine customer service to make our point. Actually, we don't know any other way to do business... and we hope you'll honor us with your order so we can prove it to you!

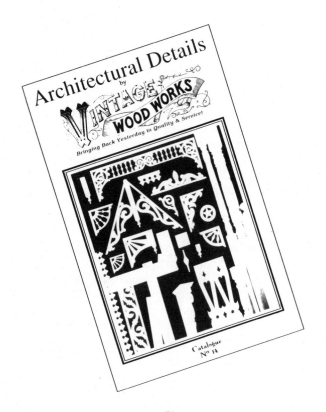

51.

The Posts

PORCH POSTS

Determine the *quantity* of Porch Posts you will need by referring to your Plan (THE POSTS, Chapter III). Note quantities for both full and Half Posts (used against walls).

Several considerations will determine the *size* (and *position* of the turned portion) of the Posts you will require. (See THE POSTS, Chapter II.) Generally, a 5" or 6" thick Post is best for residential construction, as the 4" size will appear too light. Also, over about $8^{1}/_{2}$ feet in length, a 6" thick Post will look more balanced. (Actual finished thicknesses will be less than the full inches listed above.)

The *style* of Posts you choose is a matter of personal taste.

PORCH POST MOUNTING PLATES

If Posts are allowed to sit directly on the porch floor, they will eventually get the dreaded "soggy bottom rot"! This is caused by moisture working into the space between Post and floor and then remaining for long periods of time due to limited air circulation. The solution (in addition to proper painting of the Post bottoms) is to elevate the Posts on some sort of Base Mounting Plate. You should order one Plate for each full or half Porch Post. This type of Plate is *not*, however, appropriate for Newel Posts. For Newels, see NEWEL MOUNTING KITS, below.

NEWEL POSTS

Again, consult your Plan to determine the appropriate *quantity* of Newel Posts that you will need.

Typically, Newels will be the same thickness as your Porch Posts. Their length is dictated by two factors: the length of the square *base* portion that is required for installation, and the height of the installed Handrail. We generally recommend using Newel Posts Mounting Kits, as discussed below, for the installation of your Newels. This eliminates the need for extra *base* length to accommodate the installation. Without the Mounting Kit, it will be necessary to extend the square base along the side of the structural portion of the porch to provide adequate support to the Newel. However, that method of installation could result in moisture damage to the Newel base located below the floor.

Newel length is also a matter of Handrail height. It is traditional for the *top* of the Handrail to meet the Newel one to three inches below the *top* of the flat portion of the Newel. Most Newel Posts will require some trimming to achieve this optimum length. Obviously, you'll be removing only from the *bottom* of the Newel!

NEWEL MOUNTING KITS

Newel Mounting Kits are specifically designed to provide lateral support to the Newel Posts. You will need to order one Mounting Kit for each Newel. *Please see our installation information concerning the proper use of silicon caulk for this installation.*

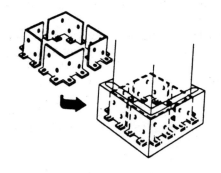

52. Our Newel Mounting Kit is a very professional way to install Newel Posts.

The Balustrade

BOTTOM RAIL

As previously discussed, we feel very strongly that **exterior installations require a Sloped-top Bottom Rail for proper water drainage**. You will need to order one length of Bottom Rail for each space that is to receive Balustrade. Since Railing is sold in even foot lengths, it is almost a certainty that you will be cutting to exact length prior to installation. Thus, it is only necessary to assure that you are ordering sufficiently long for the intended space. Remember to deduct the thickness of the Posts when determining your Rail requirements.

BALUSTERS

If you will be using Sloped-top Bottom Rails, remember that Vintage Wood Works can notch your Turned or Sawn Balusters to fit our Bottom Rail. ***Please so specify when ordering.***

Carpenters normally think in terms of "on center" spacing when installing ***Turned*** **Balusters**. That is, they want to know how far it is from the center of one Baluster to the center of the next. A very common spacing is 6" *on center*. This is partly a matter of personal taste, but if the spacing is too great, it can create sufficient space between pairs of Balusters to trap a child's head, or even to permit them to slip through. You should check your area's building code requirements on this point.

Your chosen on-center spacing probably will not work out evenly for the spaces you have to cover. If you're close, the difference can be made up by adjusting the beginning and ending Balusters. The distance from the end of the Railing to the *first* Turned Baluster center is traditionally one-half the distance from the center of one Baluster to the center of the next. However, varying your first and last Baluster center positions by more than one-half inch from the traditional "formula" could create another problem. It may be very difficult to then match the beginning spacing of the first Baluster on the other side of the Porch Post!

For those cases, the solution is to slightly change your chosen on-center spacing along the entire Balustrade. Normally, a very small increase or decrease in this distance will bring your first and last centers an acceptable distance from the ends of the Railing. A little experimentation will get it! And for you mathematicians, here's a chance for you to put your knowledge to practical use.

Despite all of the above, **it will usually work just great to determine the total length in inches of all of your Balustrade sections, and then divide this number by the on center you have chosen.** For example, let's say you have three Balustrade sections totaling 180", and you've chosen 6" for your ideal on-center spacing. Dividing 180 by 6 = 30. Thus, if you order 30 Balusters, you should have enough. (You may want to add one or two for good measure.) If you don't believe the math, get a tape measure and mark it off, remembering to start and end with one-half the on-center distance.

Sawn **Balusters** are often installed with their edges touching. This will create another pattern between each pair of Balusters. If you should choose to leave some space between each Sawn Baluster, proceed as described above for Turned Balusters, determining an on-center spacing.

Should you choose to omit any space *between* your Sawn Balusters, the question will arise as to the proper handling of Balustrade sections that require something other than a number of *full* Sawn Balusters. That is, if you have a section that is 70" long, and the Balusters are 7" each in width, then you will be using 10 complete Sawn Balusters. But, should your section be only 65" in width, it will *not* be possible to use either 9 *or* 10 full Balusters, as 65" is not divisible by 7! There are several possibilities...

The first and last Sawn Balusters in each Balustrade section do *not* have to completely fill the space right up to the Posts. However, this space should *not* be longer than one-half the width of the Baluster. If it *is* longer, then it's best to cut the first and last Baluster to fill this space. (You may use a plain piece of board of the same thickness as the Baluster to fill this space.) It is important that this space, whether filled or open, be about the same on either side of a Post, or the imbalance will be apparent. Thus, as with Turned Balusters, you must lay out each Balustrade section with adjoining sections in mind.

SUBRAIL

The use of a Subrail will, among other advantages, make Baluster installation much easier. We therefore strongly recommend its use for all porches. Subrailing should be ordered in the same lengths you have previously determined for your Bottom Rail. It must, of course, match the width of the channel in the Handrail, and *must be wide enough for your Balusters.*

HANDRAIL

And it follows, as night after day, that your Handrail channel must match the width of your Subrail! The style of Handrail is a personal choice.

Post Top Items

SPANDRELS

Since your Spandrels will occupy the same space between Porch Posts that your Balustrade sections do, they will also be of the same length. Often it is better, when using Spandrels without end cutwork, to order them a little long, and then plan on cutting to an exact fit during installation. This is especially important when the Porch Posts are *not* yet in place, since exact measurements are not yet possible.

If you choose to do this, be sure to let us know, so that we can build the Spandrels such that the first and last Ball & Dowel or Spindle will be in the right place after you trim the top and bottom framing to length.

BRACKETS

Typically, you will use two Brackets per full Porch Post (including corner Posts) , and one Bracket per half Post. If you are unsure of which *size* Bracket to order, make several cardboard "dummies". These can be simple triangular shapes, of the approximate size of the Bracket you have in mind.

Have someone hold these into place while you stand back at the curb. At this distance you may decide that a Bracket one size larger will show to better advantage. Also, try rotating your dummies 90°. You may find that you like your chosen bracket turned sideways.

Also, please consider ordering your Brackets in a thicker version, as this will greatly enhance their strength, while appearing very substantial.

RUNNING TRIMS
Since Running Trims are normally placed from Bracket to Bracket, you will need to take the horizontal measurement of the Bracket into account when determining the length of Running Trim you will need for each space. If you are using Drops to transition between Bracket and Running Trim, then also deduct their widths.

Add all of your required lengths together to arrive at the total amount of Running Trim you will need. Then, since most Running Trims are sold in fixed lengths, divide your total requirements by this fixed length, and order to the next greater whole piece of Running Trim. For example, if you determine that you will need a total of 22 feet of Trim, and if your chosen style comes in 4 foot lengths, then 22 divided by 4 equals 5.5, so you would order 6 lengths. You can then trim to fit or butt pieces together to complete each space.

Please remember that you can order your Running Trims with a moulded top rail attached. And you should also consider ordering these in a thicker version, for the reasons stated above.

BEADED RAILS
Normally, your Beaded Rails will run from Post to Post, so they should be ordered the same length as your Spandrels. *Their width should, of course, exceed the width of the bottom rail of the Spandrels.*

MEDALLIONS
In most installations, Medallions will need to be the same depth as the Spandrel. You will probably need two Medallions for each Porch Post, and one for each half Post.

Porch Eave Decoration

POST FACE BRACKETS

You will need one Post Face Bracket for each regular Porch Post, and *two* Brackets for each corner Post. It is optional whether to use a Post Face Bracket on Half Posts. As with regular Brackets, it is desirable to use cardboard "dummies" if you are unsure of which size to order.

You will definitely want to order your Post Face Brackets in a thicker material (at least 1-1/4"), since this thickness will be very prominent from most viewing angles. In fact, some prefer to use Corbels for Post Face Brackets.

BELT COURSE BRACKETS

Likewise, thickness is important for Belt Course Brackets, as their front edges will show prominently. The quantity of these Brackets you require is, of course, dependent upon how close you would like to place them, and upon how many feet of eave you have.

Once again, "dummies" can help you visualize what your Belt Course Brackets will look like when installed. In this case, it is better to get some scraps of 2 x 4 material, cut several blocks, and temporarily nail into place. Experiment with various spacings until you are satisfied.

RUNNING TRIMS AS APPLIQUES

When you plan to use Running Trim as an applique to the face of the Beam, you can deduct the thickness of Post Face and Belt Course Brackets, as the Running Trim is mounted between them. As mentioned before, most Running Trims are sold in fixed lengths, so you will need to order to the next greater whole piece of Running Trim. You can then trim to fit or butt pieces together to complete each space.

Final Thoughts

You are now well on the way to realizing that dream porch you've been wanting...

You are familiar with the various features of a porch, both structural and decorative.   More importantly, you understand how and where these components are used, and how they relate to one another and to the completed porch...

If *you* will be the one building your porch, you know many of the "tricks of the trade" that are now almost a lost art.   If someone else is to do the actual construction, you are now much better prepared to oversee and appreciate the construction process...

And perhaps most significantly, you are now ready to proceed with your project, secure in the knowledge that it will be just what you've always wanted... that graceful and peaceful retreat... that special, restful place... in short, your own *Magnificent Porch*.

Good Luck, and have a wonderful time designing, building, and *enjoying* your porch!

Final Reminders

1. We really *are* serious about porches... and we would welcome the opportunity to help you in any way we can! If questions arise, either during your reading of this book or at a later time, please give us a call at (903) 356-2158.

2. This is Book One of a two-volume set. The second book, *Magnificent Porches Manual,* tells how to professionally **install** Vintage Wood Works' porch trim, even if you're *not* a professional. We will send Book Two *free* upon request when you order any porch trim from us.

3. We'd love to see a picture of *your* Magnificent Porch. Why don't you keep a photo journal of your progress, and then send us a snapshot of the completed masterpiece?

4. We are always happy to provide a *free* quote on any custom work that you may require. It is quite easy for us to make most requested changes to our standard items, or we can work with you on designs that duplicate existing items you may need to match. We are also often asked to complete special designs for one-of-a-kind projects. Let us know how we can help.

5. But most importantly... have fun!!!

Index

Please also be aware of *two* Cross References in Chapter II (beginning on page 70). They cross reference porch components, first by specific usage, and then by Vintage Wood Works Product Number, to the porch examples shown in that chapter.

G

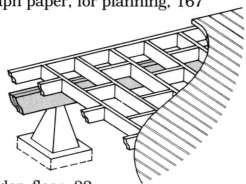

H

I

J

K

L

Porch (cont.)

R

S

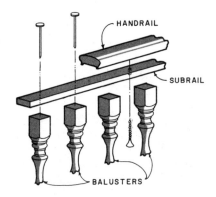

T

Transitional space, 11
Turned Balusters, 49, 183
Turned Porch Posts, 36, 181
Two-dimensional drawings, 67
Two-volume set of books, 12, 190
Two-story porch, 29

U

Usage, of porch, 15, 164

V

Verandas, 15
Vestibules, 15
Victorian period, 16
Victorian Queen Anne Style, 165
Vintage Wood Works, (903) 356-2158

W

Wall Posts. *See* Half Posts
Water drainage, 32, 35, 49, 181
Water repellant treatment, 35
Wood floors, 35

X

Y

Z

About Vintage Wood Works

For a number of years Vintage Wood Works has been at the forefront in the revival of interest in "vintage house trim". As a major supplier of old-fashioned, solid wood, handcrafted mill-work, they have worked with tens of thousands of people from all 50 states and a number of foreign countries to provide hard to find (often custom) items for the restoration and re-creation of porches, most other exterior "gingerbread", and a wide range of interior decorative millwork items.

Newly constructed homes and other buildings by the thousands have also benefited from the products of Vintage Wood Works. Numerous movie sets, Broadway productions, department stores, and specialty shops have purchased Vintage Wood Works' items for display purposes. Leading architects, designers, famous people, major entertainment theme parks, fine restaurants, commercial buildings of every variety, and major real estate developments have all incorporated Vintage's work into their plans.

But by far the largest number of shipments over the years have gone to individual homeowners throughout the country. While also working with a great many contractors, architects, and interior designers, Vintage Wood Works' primary advertising has always been directed toward the homeowner. Their ads have been seen by millions during the past 15 years in just about every home oriented magazine published.

As the first firm of its kind to advertise extensively directly to consumers (at least in the last 75 years!) Vintage Wood Works' emphasis has always been on working directly with the end user of its products. The ongoing success of this approach is evident by Vintage's position at the forefront of their industry. Their continuing endeavors in these areas are embodied in the company slogan...

Bringing Back Yesterday in Quality & Service!

The Early Years

Even prior to founding Vintage Wood Works, the author and his wife, Holly, had assembled a private collection of "Victorian Gingerbread" house trim. These items were first gathered during the mid-1970's on Gregory's business trips, during vacations, and as the opportunity arose. Attracted to the brackets, corbels, and turnings they found in salvage yards, they began to realize that perhaps others shared this interest.

In various parts of the country, pockets of interest in preserving old houses *were* evident, although marvelous Victorian mansions could still be bought very reasonably throughout the country at this time. The Victorian Revival was still a few years away, but another trend was also gaining strength; namely, the move by many away from the ultra modern and sophisticated, and back to small towns and rural lifestyles.

Thus, when the author and his wife decided to stop climbing the corporate "ladder of success" and enjoy their own *small town and rural lifestyle*, it was only natural to start a business that would reflect the "graceful and peaceful surroundings" of another time and place, to quote from the first Vintage Wood Works catalogue.

And so, in 1978, Vintage Wood Works was founded. The original concept was quite simple: Provide a better and more extensive selection of these hard-to-find items than is available locally, ship very promptly, give each and every customer the kind of personal service that is seldom available, and do all of this with real value for the dollar. This approach worked for everyone, because that early catalogue also stated that "we are happy doing what we do".

As Vintage Wood Works grew, it became an even more family oriented business. During the first few months, Gregory's brother Roland joined the business. Later his wife, Donna, also joined the business. Gregory and Roland's father, Rudolph, an ordained minister, would later retire from a lifetime in the ministry to become company Comptroller. Now at a vigorous 79, he stills comes to the office each morning, and his wife Elayne has, over the years, contributed many ideas for the business. The owners' older children have all worked in the business at various times. For all of the Tatsches it has truly been a dream come true...

... thanks to the thousands of wonderful and like-minded people from around this great country, who have worked with, bought from, and encouraged the efforts of Vintage Wood Works during the first fifteen years.

This book can be used
in tandem with the
Vintage Wood Works Catalogue,
since the various items
shown herein are all available
directly from
Vintage Wood Works.